Newsonomics

Newsonomics

TWELVE NEW TRENDS THAT WILL SHAPE THE NEWS YOU GET

KEN DOCTOR

ST. MARTIN'S PRESS ✠ NEW YORK

www.stmartins.com

Library of Congress Cataloging-in-Publication Data

Doctor, Ken.
  Newsonomics: twelve new trends that will shape the news you get / Ken Doctor. —1st ed.
      p.   cm.
    ISBN 978-0-312-59893-8
  1. Online journalism.   2. Citizen journalism.   3. Journalism—Technological innovations.   4. Journalism—Vocational guidance.   I. Title
  PN4784.062D63 2010
  070.4—dc22

                                                                              2009039691

First Edition: February 2010

10 9 8 7 6 5 4 3 2 1

To the dreamers and the schemers out there who are reinventing journalism, holding on to those conventional wisdoms that still make sense and discarding the rest

Contents

The old gatekeepers are disappearing. Now we live in a news bubble. We don't so much get the news as the news gets to us, sometimes surrounding us. We live in a world of endless choice on paper, podcast, Web, and television, so we've become our own and one another's editors.

A dozen or so multinational, multiplatform media companies will dominate global news and information. Some are broadcasters, some are cablecasters, some are newspapers, and some are wires. By 2015, though, their products will look more similar than different.

Local news companies are the hardest hit by Internet change, which has forced them to redefine themselves. They are getting much smaller and local-local-oriented as they struggle to find survival strategies. Meanwhile, city news start-ups start to grow and compete with the big boys.

11 : For Journalists' Jobs, It's Back to the Future 183

Journalists are taking a page from the history books, having to balance multiple skills and multiple gigs, to keep their heads above water.

12 : Mind the Gaps 199

We can see the blue sky of a journalism renaissance . . . but first we've got to cross a chasm of pain.

Index 209

Acknowledgments

An analyst, I've discovered, is a journalist who gets paid by someone other than a media company.

I happened on my sixth career in and around journalism quite by chance. I've been an "analyst" for almost five years and find myself extraordinarily fortunate to have a perch on the news transformation we're living through and shaping.

In retrospect, each career move seems like an internship, one building on another, some quite lucrative, others far less so. I can hardly begin to acknowledge all those I've encountered who have helped shape my thinking here.

I'd have to start, though, with this supercaffeinated news world in which we find ourselves. There's the 24/7 world of journalism, of course, and then there's the near-instantaneous and ubiquitous world of news about the news. Even before legions of journalists were given walking papers—and free time—to write about the trade, hundreds of writers, bloggers, critics, and yes, analysts had taken to the Web to comment on all things journalistic. Now, Twitter and Facebook accelerate the travel and twitch of each new thought, like a drunken pinball machine on hyperdrive.

You'll see that many of the ideas in this book have been informed by that collective ferment. It's always dangerous to name names, for concern of leaving some out that have been helpful in shaping my thinking about the evolution of news.

ACKNOWLEDGMENTS

Here, though, are some key ones.

No day would seem to start right without the requisite stops at those sites that track the news industry as we know it, though some days, the torrent is a bit daunting.

Jim Romenesko practically invented the news "weblog," and his Poynter blog is still the standard for its knowing eye on the trade and its transitions. PaidContent, invented whole by Rafat Ali and Staci Kramer, *Editor and Publisher*'s newer Fitz and Jen blog, and AllThingsD are must-reads. Among other sites, the Online News Association's Cyberjournalist, the World Association of Newspapers' Editor's Weblog, Mark Glaser's MediaShift, the Nieman Journalism Lab site Mousetrap Media's Journalism.co.uk, Silicon Alley Insider, Pew's Internet and American Life Project, TechCrunch and Mashable, all demand attention. WNYC's *On the Media* is an indispensable weekly listen.

Then, there are the individual commentators—making sense of the changes, advocates for thinking, and thinking differently, about the emerging news media landscape. They are all part of this astounding conversation moving us forward. Again, at the risk of missing a few, let me include these: John Battelle, Cory Bergman, John Blossom, Angela Connor, Vin Crosbie, Rick Edmonds, Dan Gillmor, Barry Graubart, Roy Greenslade, Alan Jacobson, Jeff Jarvis, Peter Krasilovsky, Alan Mutter, Peter Preston, Scott Rosenberg, Michael Miner, Steve Outing, Mark Potts, Jay Rosen, Steve Rubel, Jack Shafer, Clay Shirky, Greg Sterling, John Temple, Amy Webb, David Westphal, Fred Wilson, and Steve Yelvington.

We build on each other's ideas, engage in intellectual battles, and offer the odd edit that solo writers often need so badly.

The news press has had a hell of a time covering itself, lately succumbing to some news fatigue about its own faltering fortunes. It's the familiar problem about news: how do you tell a fresh story about news—in this case, unrelenting downsizing—that lacks "fresh" angles? I've enjoyed my back-and-forth with media reporters. Whether from Berlin, Baltimore, or Bangalore, they are trying to tell this essential story of our times, and I often gain insights in my talks with them.

I also want to thank my clients, both those that I've served in ongoing relationships and project-based ones as well. They do more than pay the bills; they keep me engaged in the real-life strategic and tactical decisions of the times.

My work with Outsell is particularly noteworthy. A half-decade ago, Outsell CEO Anthea Stratigos and I met to talk about covering the news industry for her company that has long set a standard of coverage about information industry publishers more widely. I told her I didn't really want to be an employee or an employer in my next career stage, and we scoped out a plan. We've tweaked it along the way, with great mutual results. Thanks to her and all my Outsell colleagues who continue to teach me great lessons, some of which the news industry can adapt from such fields as trade, science, education, and medical publishing.

An analyst's work is spent online, in travel, and on the phone. I've talked to hundreds of people in the last several years, those recently out of newsrooms, those in start-ups and bigger emerging companies and those in transition. They've patiently answered my calls and e-mails, offering their perspectives and insights. An analyst couldn't do the job without them and, of course, can't name them, given the often-requested need for confidentiality.

You know who you are. Thank you all.

I also want to thank here the more than dozen people in the business who took some time to specifically answer questions posed in this book, and whose replies I've included to round out most of the Newsonomics laws. All have high to-do piles, and their time is precious.

Though my Knight Ridder experience of twenty-one years is fast slipping into history, I see how the hundreds of people within that company who I got to know well shaped my perspective on the business of news. Knight Ridder, for many years, was easily the silver standard in the industry, lacking the cachet of the *Times* and the *Post,* but speaking to a way of doing journalism right. Becoming a Knight Ridder editor meant something.

Among a few to note: Jim Batten, late KR CEO, who stayed late at work one evening long ago to convince me to stay with the company and promised career-making opportunities in the years ahead. Soon after, Saint Paul Pioneer Press editor Deborah Howell met me at the Twin Cities airport. We immediately hit it off and remain friends today.

The biggest Deborah lesson (and many of us have a number of these memorized): when you're an editor with lots of responsibilities to your readers and staff, listen for the voice in the back of your head. If that voice is nagging you to double-check, or revisit, or rethink, don't ignore it. A great journalism lesson, a great life lesson, well-used.

Her successor, Walker Lundy, promoted me to managing editor. A Southern fish *seemingly* out of water in the true north of Minnesota, his homespun aphorisms often masked his deep insight. One time he said to me: "You know, Ken, I expect things to go wrong, and when they don't, I'm pleasantly surprised. You expect things to go right, and when they don't [too often in a newsroom] you're disappointed."

That comment didn't make me check my eternal optimism at the door, but sometimes temper it with, shall we say, realism.

Much of that KR career was built on my formative years in Oregon, first as publisher and editor of the Eugene-based *Willamette Valley Observer* alternative weekly. I see lots of parallels between those days and the emergence of the green sprouts of online journalism today.

Those early Eugene days were formative, too, because of my graduate journalism education at the University of Oregon. I gained pointers there that I still use as an analyst decades later. Lately, I've been fortunate to reconnect with the UO Journalism School, through Dean Tim Gleason, one of the nation's pioneers in reinventing journalism education in the digital age.

None of these experiences would have been as possible, of course, without my family. My wife Kathy is an uncommon source of common sense in all things, professional and personal. She believes that if everyone paid attention just a bit more, the world would be a better place. She's right.

I now grok another reason to become a father. If you're fortunate to sustain a career after your children become productive adults, you learn new things from them all the time, which further inform your work.

I joke that I'm the only one in the family working for profit-making companies, and that maybe a 1:4 ratio is a good one, there. Kathy, Jenika, Katy, and Joe all have done work around service, working for nonprofits. In their work in health care, fisheries ecology, global study, and education reform, they provide a stream of reminders about the value of good journalism to our communities and the wider world. As part of a generation that grew up with the early Internet, their digital preferences and creations have been eye-opening and their feedback to my work invaluable. Jenika's edits on this book early on set me on the right path.

For revealing a few of the mysteries of book publishing, I owe my agent, Bill Gladstone of Waterside Productions. Bill knows every byway of the book business and found the ideal editor.

Phil Revzin at St. Martin's Press has been a godsend. Phil is a wise head. He's a rare deep veteran of the trade, through a long and distinguished career at *The Wall Street Journal,* who understands and grasps the transformation upon us. His guidance to a first-time book author has been timely and to the point—and those are values that endure as we move from one era to the next.

Newsonomics

PROLOGUE
Sweethearts, Get Me Rewrite

In 2009, journalism almost seemed to rewrite itself. We saw an unprecedented—if not unexpected—shrinking of the press. Long-standing business models blew apart. Many publishers tried to put a prettier face on it, calling it realignment, restructuring, new strategic directions, all of which sounded better than "panic."

Panic it was, though, as at least another four thousand journalists were tossed out of American newsrooms, while the rest had no time for survivor's guilt. They had their pay cut, their retirement contributions frozen, and their workweeks reduced by furloughs. Worse yet, many were forced to cover the diminishing of their own paper or trade.

Only the readers—all of us—fared worse.

It's not your eyes that are deceiving you. We're getting less news.

There are simply far fewer people bringing it to us. Overall, America's daily newspapers have shed about ten thousand newsroom jobs in the last decade, well down from the 2001 peak of 56,400. While we can sympathize with the 45,000 or so journalists who remain under stress in U.S. newsrooms, how do we begin to comprehend the loss of their reporting, of their community knowledge?

Newspapers have been sliced and diced down to near-brochure size. Almost a hundred of America's dailies are no longer daily, an oxymoron if there ever was one. Many stories are never covered. There are simply fewer reporters available to cover them.

So we know less. How much less? We don't know exactly, but we do have some indications. Over the last five years, U.S. newspaper companies have cut their newsprint usage by 40 percent. Figure that half of what has been cut is ads and half news. So the 20 percent cut in newsroom staff is about matched by a 20 percent cut in news reporting. Other numbers give us a glimpse of the vast changes we're seeing, as noted in "Newsonomics 101: The News Revolution by the Numbers," below.

NEWSONOMICS 101: The News Revolution by the Numbers

- In the first quarter of 2009, Google—the leading search company—saw *profits* of $1.4 billion. In the same period, Gannett—the leading news company—reported *total revenue* of $1.4 billion, and profits of only $58 million.
- Yahoo, MSNBC, AOL, and CNN make up four of the top five news sites in the country; *The New York Times* is the only newspaper company in the top five.
- Forty percent of Americans now cite the Internet as a daily news source for national and global news, topping newspapers (at 35 percent) for the first time, in a Pew study. Preeminent, though, is still TV, at 70 percent. Among those under thirty, 59 percent choose the Internet as their chief source.
- American daily newspapers cut at least 8,000 newsroom jobs in the last two years alone.
- The last time daily newspaper circulation increased was in 1984, when it peaked at an average of 63.3 million papers per day. Now it is down to about 43 million papers a day.
- U.S. dailies saw an advertising revenue peak of $49 billion in 2000. In 2009, they earned about $28 billion from ads.
- The average age of a network evening news viewer: 63. The average age of a newspaper reader: 57.
- U.S. teens watch TV 60 percent less than their parents and spend 600 percent more time online than their parents.
- Thirty-two U.S. newspapers maintained their own Washington bureaus last year, half as many as in the 1980s.

- **Non-U.S. media are expanding their American presence.** *The Guardian* has set up a five-person bureau in Washington, D.C. The BBC's staff of fifty is one-third larger than four years ago, and Al-Jazeera's staff includes more than one hundred.

It's not only the United States that is seeing the newspaper decline; it's a phenomenon of the developed world. Though European and Japanese newspapers get more of their revenue from readers and subscribers than their U.S. counterparts, they're seeing the same advertising losses. They are cutting down the size of their products and staffs as well, though not as dramatically as U.S. companies. Even French president Nicolas Sarkozy has declared a press emergency.

With all these cutbacks, it's hard to put a finger on exactly what we're no longer getting.

In short, we don't know what we don't know, but we do know we know less than we used to.

It's a time to despair and pack it in, right?

Well, no, it's not. That's not a luxury we have.

What we do have is the opportunity to rewrite the news about the news.

Almost hidden in the news-as-we-know-it collapse is another story.

We are on the brink of the Digital News Decade. Just as we start the millennium's second decade, we embark upon a new news era. It is popping out everywhere, from small start-ups in San Diego, the Twin Cities, and New Haven to truly global, multimedia news companies like CNN, Reuters, and Bloomberg. We're even seeing a time when the old Gray Lady of print, *The New York Times*, wins the pinnacle of broadcast awards—the Peabody—and CNN, once a cable upstart, gets into the news wire business, churning out, well, text stories. That's why we now have to use the word "text" to describe the written words. "Print" is a term that's going the way of the buggy whip.

The second decade of the twenty-first century will truly be a Digital News Decade, just as the first has been one of profound transformation. We've seen the emergence of newspaper companies that are mostly print with a little digital and of broadcast companies that have dipped their toes into the online waters; in the next decade, all these companies will become mainly digital, holding on to vestiges of their former selves. Yes, newspapers and evening news broadcasts may well survive, but they'll be a tail that no longer wags the dog.

Overall, my sense is that we are closer to the end of the beginning than to the beginning of the end of this particular news revolution. "Newspapers" may well be going the road taken by "record albums," "transistor radios," or "appointment TV." The news, however, stops for no one.

Instead, this is a new hybrid age of news(papers). It took years before the Prius got the hybrid model right and emerged as standard, the model against which the next generation of hybrids is being judged. The hybrid news era—lots more digital, some print—is just forming, and we've not yet found our Prius.

It's certainly been an ungainly time of death and of birth. There are those who can barely contain their joy at the cratering of old media as they warmly embrace Web 2.0 News and beyond. I call them the fire-and-rain crowd as in James Taylor's anthemic, "I've seen fire and I've seen rain. . . . Sweet dreams and flying machines in pieces on the ground." Then, there are those who believe old media's passing means the end of Western Civilization As We Know It.

The truth, as it often does, lies somewhere between. Much undoubtedly has been lost, but much will be gained.

I've titled this book *Newsonomics*, and it's a snapshot of a fast-changing industry, circa 2010. News and economics are the two big issues, quite simply: How do we get the news produced? How do we pay for it? Despite all the ink and pixels expended on the changing world of news, too little has been made of the building blocks of the future and of how their business models will work.

Newsonomics is not a book of media criticism. We can—and do daily—debate the splendid highs and lurid lows of the business of journalism. That debate will rage on no matter how much or how little journalism we produce. *Newsonomics* is focused on the key trends that will determine who indeed brings us the news and what we're likely to get. I've tried to keep as much jargon out of these pages as possible so that smart readers—outside as well as inside the industry—can make sense of the changing times.

From my work as a news industry analyst, I've distilled what I think are the Twelve Laws of Newsonomics, principles that are determining what's being created and by whom.

These Twelve Laws aren't a kit, with a step-by-step instruction manual. They are really a set of building blocks. I think of them as a set of really cool Legos, blocks that can morph into many kinds of news businesses and organizations. We can see some of these structures, all very much in progress, but know that we aren't yet seeing a finished city of news, just lots of villages. How well editors, marketers, and publishers combine and recombine these laws—there's new news DNA in process—will determine their success or failure. In that vein, I'll highlight cross-links between points and chapters, reinforcing the notion that these Twelve Laws really are interconnected building blocks of the new news business. It's not quite Web hyperlinking, but the best we can do with ink on paper.

Now with the business model of the newspaper (and, right behind it, of broadcast news) busted, one big question is how much influence will be exerted by whoever pays for the news in the years ahead. We'll look at this question as we move through our Twelve Laws. Someone always pays for the news, and that support has always spawned debates about who news organizations favor or fear. Clearly, in the United States, it has long been advertisers, who paid most of the cost (80 percent) of producing the news. And, yes, car dealers could launch a revenue-draining boycott of the local paper from time to time, when they got testy about coverage. For the most part, though, having a large and diverse set of advertisers meant that newspapers could largely do their work without much pressure.

In this new era, we will end up getting the journalism that we as a society and individuals pay for. While advertising long paid for large local newsrooms of several hundred professional snoops, that funding appears to have been a happy historical accident. Jim Batten, once CEO of Knight Ridder, my journalistic home for twenty-one years, told us back in 1988 that the "institution of American journalism owes more to the institution of the department store than the First Amendment." He said it matter-of-factly, to the shock of then-assembled top Knight Ridder editors. We all would have liked to believe that our vast resources were somehow Constitutional, but his blunt realism gave us great pause. Now his words have proven terribly true.

As department stores have folded and consolidated and cut greatly back on advertising, newspapers have seen their own fortunes wane as well. God, apparently, didn't ordain that newspapers would forever be able to pay good, middle-class, civil-service wages to hundreds of journalists in every city. Certainly, in this nation of 300 million, in the richest nation on the face of the earth and in the history of the world, we can figure out how to pay living wages to fifty thousand or so people who root out what's going on in our communities and cities.

As new business models develop, so are new ways of thinking about the production of news. Newspaper companies are exploring the power of audio and video storytelling. Local broadcasters are training staff to write text stories. In Law No. 11, we'll look at the new skill sets needed by both fresh-out-of-college journalists and midcareer newsies.

Newsonomics takes a hardheaded look forward, while also explaining how we've ended up in this situation today. Law No. 4, "The Old News World Is Gone. Get Over It," gives you a good sense of how we got to this point. Ultimately, though, I—and I think it is true for all of us—am most interested in figuring out how we move ahead rather than in performing an autopsy.

How can I write a forward-looking book, given the carnage we've seen? My thinking is that we have no choice. Being pro-journalism means being pro-information and pro-knowledge. Having been part of the journalism sausage-making factories, I know it can be an often unpleasant process. But there's no doubt that in our struggling little democracy, information and knowledge are like the air we breathe—absolutely needed—and we're feeling a bit thin on that right now. We have no choice but to be optimistic and support the best journalism we can.

This new journalism is discordant, more like a cacophony of voices than the sonorous choruses we grew up with. Just as Timothy

Crouse's seminal *The Boys on the Bus* captured reporter groupthink, we now see ourselves emerging from the age of conformist dailies. Often, as we have travelled from city to city, too much of the daily press seems boring, almost generic. Old monopoly journalism—now encumbered by debt—has found itself encrusted with habit, traditional ways of doing things that worked well for decades and then failed when they failed to adapt to new realities.

Now there's a blooming, buzzing confusion out there, to borrow a William James phrase from the turn of the (twentieth) century, and I love it.

The Internet age has given readers and journalists alike unbelievable new tools to produce and distribute the news, and to read it anywhere and everywhere, and from the greatest diversity of sources imaginable. That promise remains, even as a mundane, but fundamental, question persists: Who is going to pay for the creation of high-quality news?

Importantly, *Newsonomics* isn't just about the upcoming winners and losers; it's also about the values that define the new landscape. The business of news—unlike soap-selling, auto-offering or pill-peddling—is unlike any other business. It balances profit-making and public service at its core. Citizens across the globe depend on the business of news to find out what's going on. Who brings us the news matters.

Press critic A. J. Liebling once famously wrote that "freedom of the press is guaranteed only to those who own one." In an age when production and distribution is nearly free, we're rewriting that history. It's no longer about owning the means of production, but producing new means to old ends. It's about re-creating a vibrant press for the next era of American history.

This book, then, is intended to be a handbook for all those who care deeply about our news future—the dreamers, the schemers, the planners, the strategists, the investors, and, yes, the readers.

So let's wade into this new news ocean, and the look at the first law as we consider the unexpected world of news choice now sprawled out in front of us.

1

In the Age of Darwinian Content,
You Are Your Own Editor

It's amazing that the amount of news that happens in the world every day always just exactly fits the newspaper.—**JERRY SEINFELD, comedian**

Control your *own* destiny *or* someone else will.—**JACK WELCH, magnate**

You used to be able to count your daily news sources on one hand. If you were the average American, you read your daily newspaper, watched the evening news, and subscribed to several magazines. In the car, maybe, you caught some news on the radio.

It's not for nothing that Walter Cronkite and Chet Huntley and David Brinkley were household words to my parents' generation. These guys weren't talking heads. They were editors. Along with their staffs, they picked what they thought we needed to know that evening. And then packed it neatly into thirty minutes. Weekends, well, that was leisure time. News happened Monday to Friday.

Newspaper editors played the same role.

In 1994, I became managing editor of the *Saint Paul Pioneer Press*, a daily of about 200,000 circulation in the Twin Cities, with more than two hundred people working in the newsroom. Managing editor, as in M.E., as in the second-ranking editor. A key M.E. responsibility: making a final decision on what went on Page One the next morning. At first, it was both exhilarating and anxiety producing.

Knowing that the pick I'd ratify would determine what some 400,000 readers saw first thing the next morning gave pause.

I was a gatekeeper.

Today the familiar gatekeepers—top editors at daily papers, those who put together the evening news broadcasts—have lost their audiences and their sway. Those newspaper gatekeepers used to bring their readers the world—national news, international news, business news, sports news, entertainment news, and local news. Now it's that last area—local—that may be their refuge from the Internet storm.

For decades, more than 1,500 daily newspapers—most of them, chain-owned—created their own national pages, their own world pages, their own business pages, their own national entertainment pages. Sure, corporate offices tried pushing economies of scale, suggesting pages that were centrally produced, at far less cost. Most local editors rebelled, though, and the work most industries would consider redundant stayed in place for a long time.

"We'll tell our readers what's important," local editors bellowed. In fact, for all the editor concentration and cost, readers were getting a bit of *New York Times* lite, *Washington Post* lite, and *Los Angeles Times* lite, plus a smattering of AP and other newswires. Readers—that's you—are no dummies and figured it out, once technology released the stranglehold of local editors. Why take your local editors' edited, truncated-for-print versions of *The New York Times*, *The Washington Post*, the *Los Angeles Times*, and hundreds of other complete sources? Why settle for *New York Times* lite from your local paper?

Why, indeed? And so, many of us have migrated, at least for part of what we need to know, from the daily print paper to Internet news reading. In fact, not just many, but most. As 2008 closed, the well-regarded Pew Research Center told us that the Internet had surpassed newspapers as a national and international news source for the first time. (See "Newsonomics 101: The News Revolution by the Numbers," page 2.)

The Internet brought that level of change in one quick decade, in less than one generation. Now readers can get the full-bore report of all of those publications and much, much more, if they know where to look (usually Yahoo, Google, and the like), *for free.*

That's why we start with Law No. 1: In the Age of Darwinian Content, You Are Your Own Editor. We have now become our own gatekeepers; we no longer see the news world as a gated community.

We live in a news bubble. We don't so much get the news as the news gets to us, sometimes surrounding us. At work, in our cars, at home—and even in elevators and at gas pumps. It's now hard *not* to know what's going on.

News of actor Heath Ledger's death, in January 2006, traveled at the speed of the Web, the very definition of viral news. One friend told me he was amazed when his grandmother e-mailed him the news!

Now, we move among formerly separate worlds—print and broadcast, news and features, news and blogs, the deadly serious and the deadly funny—effortlessly.

We can pick from *The New York Times* or *The Dallas Morning News* or the *Chicago Tribune*. We can watch CNN or ABC or listen to NPR's *All Things Considered* or Ira Glass's fine feature journalism on *This American Life* when we have the time to tune in. Agence France Presse and Reuters bring us coverage from around the world, and the BBC, *The Economist*, and *The Guardian* reverse a couple of hundreds of years of history and recolonize America with their reporting. The blogosphere can deliver dozens of viewpoints daily, with the Huffington Post targeting progressives as Red State targets conservatives.

Miss the *NewsHour with Jim Lehrer*, want to catch Rachel Maddow's show, or need to catch up on the latest antinews with Stewart and Colbert? Do it online when you want to. All that and reams more get tossed together, mixed and matched, endlessly, through each twenty-four hours.

Key to this news revolution is a huge change: We've leapt from a point of scarcity—readers could only get to so much news and information, depending on their budget and where they lived—to a point of near universal and largely free access. Similarly, advertisers, who used to have to compete for scarce placements to reach us consumers, can now choose from a nearly infinite "inventory." That produces this irony: The scarcity-to-plenty transformation that gives consumers great choice has limited news producers' ability to provide that choice.

How do we get a sense of the news production that we have lost? It's easiest to see in individual stories that may never have been published. (See "Newsonomics 101: The Impact of 828,000 Stories *Not* Published," below.)

NEWSONOMICS 101: The Impact of 828,000 Stories *Not* Published

We can figure that local communities across the United States have already lost at least 20 percent of their reporting.

Yet what has been lost is, of course, hard to put your finger on.

When *The Boston Globe* was threatened with shutdown in spring 2009, even the usually *Globe*-contentious *Boston Phoenix* pointed out what would be lost if the *Globe* really vanished: The *Globe*, it said, had "Boston's only full-time religion reporter, 5 health and science reporters, 36 metro reporters, 122 reporters total in its newsroom. . . . [and] produces good, sometimes great work that dominates the local conversation." The *Phoenix* scribe added: "It's true that the *Globe*'s demise would create major opportunities for other news outlets, including the *Phoenix*. But even as a group, it would be exceedingly difficult for the rest of us to fill the post-*Globe* vacuum."

We got another very specific view of what's lost when, at the end of February 2009, the 150-year-old *Rocky Mountain News* closed its doors. Gone. No "online only." No *Rocky* in any form.

WNYC's *On the Media,* the best media criticism show out there, answered the most important question: So just what might the readers miss, with the *Rocky* gone? After all, *The Denver Post* is still publishing, right?

Here's an excerpt from a March 6, 2009, interview between *On the Media* host Brooke Gladstone and *Rocky* reporter Laura Frank:

BROOKE GLADSTONE: So, what stories were you working on the week the paper went under?

LAURA FRANK: What would have been in our Saturday paper, the first paper that the *Rocky* missed because of its closure? We had stories ready to go about a government agency that had allegedly misused public money, we had a story about how children in state custody were being abused. And we had a story about a bus driver in Denver who was helping an elderly lady and her daughter across the street when he was hit by another vehicle, and the State Patrol gave him a ticket for jaywalking. Our reporter was ready to write that the bus driver was actually in the legal crosswalk; he should never have been given the ticket at all.

BROOKE GLADSTONE: Were these stories being covered by the—forgive me—*Denver Post*?

LAURA FRANK: In this case, no, none of these stories have been covered by the other media.

Let's take Laura Frank's quick list of three stories done by four reporters on one day. Now let's do a little multiplication, and we'll need a calculator. Let's start with the number 8,300, the official number of newsroom jobs cut in 2007–2008, according to the American Society of News Editors. Now, let's say two-thirds—5,520—of those positions were reporters, writers, and columnists, each of the positions (reporting and editing) helping to produce 150 stories a year. That's 828,000 stories a year. Each year. Neither written nor read.

Laura Frank's words ring in our ears because those are specific stories that would have appeared in an edition never published. It's harder to think about a million or so stories a year that we know nothing about.

CONSIDER:

• Yahoo News has long been among the top news sites in the United States. Yahoo was the first to figure out that people wanted choice. If you want to see a variety of takes on a new administration policy or the starlet disaster story du jour, enter a few words into a search box, and you're likely to get 367 or more responses. Search engines are agnostic about geography, as well, with news from Raleigh, Rome, and Rawalpindi equally clickable.

- New news brands and bylines have sprung up seemingly over-night. Sites like Politico, the Huffington Post, Slate, and Salon all have large devoted followings, while thousands of niche sites of lesser size have regular and sizable audiences.

- Missed ABC's *This Week* or NPR's *Morning Edition?* Time-shift, watching and listening when *you* want at the click of a mouse.

- We've moved from having only U.S.-centric choices to worldwide choices. While many newspapers have cut back coverage in their Washington, D.C., bureaus, worldwide media have ramped up; the BBC's staff of fifty is one-third larger than it was in 2005. Arab cablecaster Al-Jazeera hosts a staff of more than one hundred. Overall, 796 media outlets from 113 countries now have offices in the nation's capital, compared with 507 outlets from 79 countries in 1994, according to the Project for Excellence in Journalism.

- News video is now mainstream. At least half of Americans watch news video at least monthly. Already one quarter watch video on their phones, though that number includes YouTube entertainment fodder as well as "news."

- Blogs are a key part of our news diet. One in four Americans reads blogs at least weekly, according to research conducted at Outsell, for whom I serve as an analyst.

Consider how many times a day you get e-mail messages, or Tweets, or Facebook wall postings with suggested links to news sto-ries or blog posts or podcasts or Web reports of one kind or another. RSS readers can turn streams of news into a big, endlessly flowing river. We can be inundated with news alerts delivered to our e-mail, e-mails delivered to our phones, phones that beep or play marimbas at the sound of any incoming information. It can all be overwhelm-ing, but it's the world we are creating.

It's not so strange. It's just like olden village word of mouth, mag-nified by what I like to think of as the magic of our time, what I call prestidigitization. Technology has unshackled news from its physical packages—a newspaper, a catch-it-once-or-else radio show, or a TV newscast—and preserved it and let it free, as we'll explore deeper in Law No. 7.

While traditional command-and-control media, like daily newspapers and broadcast news certainly maintain strong, if diminished, gatekeeping functions, think of the other gates, though, that have opened for all of us. Among them: blogs, podcasts, Twitter feeds, Facebook scrawls, LinkedIn messages, satellite radio, niched cable news, and news parody that's often really news itself. Those are some of the new sources, and they are mediated weakly. Sometimes, we fetch them ourselves, but often we now get our news and information touts from the people we know.

So on the one hand, we've become free agents, choosing our own news. On the other, we've become each other's editors. We fulfill the functions that those daily anchors and editors used to do. It's lots more ungainly, less well-packaged, and harder to summarize at the day's end.

In an average day, we still consume about as much news as we did a decade ago, about sixty minutes a day. The counters, though, now have a hell of a hard time counting. Not only do we have more choice, but we've become a nation of news multitaskers, taking in radio or Internet audio while taking care of the kids or working.

If we're spending about the same amount of time consuming news, and we have a lot more choice, then we have a situation in which infinite news confronts scarce time.

And so we come to the notion of Darwinian content. Those old-time gatekeepers used to decide what part of the news to which they had access would be made available to us readers. About 10 percent of the incoming wire news at a daily newsroom made it into print; the rest, never to be read, disappeared into the ether.

Now we individually have almost infinite news choice. We are unshackled from the physical limitations of old-world newspaper and broadcast delivery. Our time, though, is still limited. So the fight is on: Which news content wins and which loses?

Talk about survival of the fittest. Only the fittest news will make the cut.

What constitutes fit? We're still working that out.

In a war of Darwinian content, it's not just the best content that will win. It's not a meritocracy. News-producing companies that adapt best and quickest will win. Certainly journalistic quality has something to do with those prospects. As important, though, is how well the news companies creating the content have adapted to the ways of the Web. In this book, we'll see that the emerging winners are those companies that are learning how to use technology better than the other guys, how to engage the social nature of Web news reading and response, how to focus their offerings to specific audiences, and, of course, how to sell advertising related to the news.

Those that excel will win: That's the stuff we'll be reading and watching. Those that fail the Internet transition test will follow the New York *Herald Tribune* or *Life* magazine or the Mutual Broadcasting System into oblivion.

Think of it, maybe, as an extension of the Reality Show era that has transformed TV. It's our new News Reality Show, in which the sharp-elbowed players—some we may like, some we may detest—use every means to win. With great frequency, someone gets kicked off the island. That's the new news world, which is no longer staid and steady. It seems no one is more than a few steps away from being pushed into the sea.

Consider that we're at the beginning of this choice revolution. When we began reading news on the Internet in the midnineties, we were tethered to large, bulky desktop computers. We went to the only available digital reading source. Now we can take all manner of reading sources with us. First, the portable laptop joined the desktop. Now, though, we've got iPhones, Kindles, Sony Readers, and this year a slew of new more-paperlike screens will emerge.

Will these choices include the good old ink-on-paper product? The short answer is yes, for a while, in most but not all cities and towns. You'll be paying for it the way you pay for a Starbucks coffee, though closer to a Starbucks price than the quarter a newspaper used to cost. You'll be buying a niche product, made for those (mostly baby boomers and up in age) who prize the comfort, habit, and feel of newsprint.

Yes, the printed newspaper is obsolescent, but our on-the-move reading choices are multiplying rapidly. In fact, most of these new devices are intended for us as consumers of news, information, and entertainment. Compare that to the desktops and laptops; those were machines—"computers"—aimed at helping us produce things. So, long way around, we're moving back to products, like newspapers, that are about us as consumers.

As consumers in this new land, we must become much more selective, exercising judgment that we couldn't exercise before. That means that we may decide we can find better news and information than that delivered to us through the familiar local newspaper or local TV station. That means content competes in ways it never did before.

Take just one familiar area in which we see the Darwinian content principle at work, movie reviews. Any daily paper of size and substance, of course, used to have its own movie reviewer; that was just the way it was. If you were the editor of the paper, you would hire the best critics you could—and if it was a union paper, that choice might stick around longer than you ever imagined—and then that person's standing was often assured for years.

Back in the 1980s, when I told our movie reviewer at the *Pioneer Press* that we were going to add a four-star rating system to all reviews, she protested that if we provided such a shorthand system, readers wouldn't be forced to read her reviews!

Flash forward, and now the readers are in charge here. At Metacritic or Rotten Tomatoes, readers can find aggregated all the top newspaper and broadcast reviews and those of independent critics. We've gotten used to the value of aggregation, as I will discuss in chapter 5.

Those movie-rating stars? They've morphed into a 100-point rating system that provides an at-a-glance comparison of what America's critics everywhere think about what's best in the theaters.

That local newspaper film critic? He has lost his job, or been laid off, or is now covering local news. The Internet eliminated the semimonopoly newspaper film critics had on their readers' attention. Again, it's the democratization of reading, as only the best local critics may survive. Whoever we as readers deem the fittest of the film critics will survive and get paid for their craft.

What's true of film critics is as true of TV critics, national and global news editors, travel section editors, and many more. What they do can now be found, quickly and easily, elsewhere.

So, in the world of almost infinite choice, how do we best exercise these judgments as readers?

Well, at first, it can appear to be an ocean of news out there, endless water with few buoys marking the way.

After all, no one yet has come up with an iTunes for the news, one simple interface that would bring the world of news choices to us and give us tools to manage and organize, rate and sort, download and listen.

Instead we have the first-generation news aggregators, like Yahoo News and Google News. They are fairly ugly, with little sense of hierarchy or style, but they do bring us links to many of more than four thousand news sources on a single page. It's similar to the abysmal online cable guides that we endure, a poor way to sort the bounty of cable offerings.

In part, no surprise, we find new gatekeepers. After things fall apart, we reassemble them. We find collectors or, in contemporary parlance, curators, of news that we like.

Just as previous generations depended on the Ben Bradlees, the Walter Cronkites, and the Paul Harveys, news consumers are starting to find gatekeepers with whom they are comfortable. Some are familiar holdovers: the editors at *The New York Times*, *Time*, or *The Washington Post*, and at their local daily, reduced though they may be in impact. Some are newer faces, a number of whom you will meet in these pages: Marketplace's Kai Ryssdal, New West's Jonathan Weber, Seattle *P-I*'s Michelle Nicolosi, Fox's Bill O'Reilly, MinnPost's Joel Kramer, Salon's Joan Walsh, the Big Money's Jim Ledbetter, Huffington Post's Arianna Huffington, and paidContent's Rafat Ali.

Though the Web allows us to be our own editors, the truth is most of us like the opinion and judgment of others—editors, in the old parlance.

In addition to those editors, we've got a new source providing judgment on what's worth reading. Let's call them recommenders. Increasingly, we rely on friends and associates to find the odd story or the highly meaningful one and send it our way. Those are the e-mail messages, or Tweets, or Facebook touts offering a seductive link. Then there are the recommenders we've never met, the wisdom of the masses, those who make the "most e-mailed story" boxes one of the most-used features on any news site. Following the links can give you a pretty good daily education.

If it seems a bit different, a bit strange, think about how we found out stuff long before computers, indeed before electricity. Word of mouth. It's as old as people living together in communities. People passed along news, warnings, tips, gossip, and whatever else interested them. Some towns employed criers to let everyone in on the news. All that the Internet represents—with its immediacy and funny brand names—is superheated word of mouth.

Almost all of us are used to following links these days, but as in all things Web, it is the young who often lead us. Observers noticed the Obama campaign's early savvy about the viral spread of information. For instance, after George W. Bush delivered his last State of the Union address, in January 2008, then Senator Barack Obama gave the Democratic response on TV. In the old days, the news would have ended there. One broadcast, followed by the next-day reporting of it.

Obama's people, though, immediately posted the response on YouTube, and it was soon watched more than an additional million times, with more than five hundred blogs and an uncountable number of e-mail links to it. Remember Katie Couric's interviews with Sarah Palin during the 2008 campaign? (See "Newsonomics 101: The Couric/Palin Web Primer," page 20.) After broadcast, those interviews pulled in more viewers online than on air, passed along to others by *us*.

NEWSONOMICS 101: The Couric/Palin Web Primer

CBS News Anchor Katie Couric's interviews with Sarah Palin were influential in forming public opinion about the Alaskan governor. One-on-one interviewing—echoes of *Frost/Nixon*—once again proved that an age-old technique can be decisive, even in the digital age.

Curiously, we saw the impact of the interviews, though strong in the initial broadcasts, *most* strongly in their viral sharing on the Web.

The broadcasts drew about 6 million viewers for the week. (In their heyday network news broadcasts drew two and three times those numbers.) Those same Couric-Palin interviews drew more than 8 million viewers online. Only 15 percent, though, of those viewers saw them on CBSNews.com, with various pirated copies drawing the most viewers through YouTube and other sources.

So let's look at the Newsonomics of that shift.

Let's estimate that CBS can charge about $30 for each one thousand viewers, a good average for a "pre-roll" ad on a nationally branded interview. If CBS had made money from each of about the 1.5 million viewers on its own site with a pre-roll (it runs spots before some news videos, but not each one), it would have earned about $45,000. If CBS could have monetized all 8 million or so views, that number would increase to $240,000.

Let's compare that to what CBS earns on air. We can estimate that Katie Couric's third-rated newscast charges about $40,000 for each of its sixteen or so thirty-second ads, or about $640,000 in all for each night's show. (On average, thirty-minute programs carry eight minutes of commercials.)

So, circa 2008, in the early days of an immature video ad market, we see how much money the Web could have provided CBS if it had protected itself from piracy and, indeed, the networks have been getting better at reclaiming their news product over the past year.

Yes, the broadcast dollars still are a lot larger than the online

(*continued*)

dollars. But broadcast audiences—with an average age of sixty— are diminishing steadily. Online audiences and online ad video are maturing rapidly.

Take the Couric-Palin interviews as an early lesson. To the extent broadcasters, especially those with global reach, can harness valuable segments of their news production and let it loose, attached to advertising, around the Web and around the globe, they've got huge, new opportunity to move on.

Traditionalists often decry the serendipity lost in the Internet age—you just never knew what you would discover in all those daily newspaper pages. We see the surprise in the I-never-would-have-searched-for-that-story e-mail sent to us by friends, and when we like it, we pass it on.

Those traditionalists forget a key point. While readers accepted journalistic gatekeepers for many years, they never quite trusted them. In survey after survey over the years, journalists have found themselves near the bottom of the "Who Do You Trust?" charts. Ahead of them were doctors, teachers, cops, judges, and, until the 2008 financial meltdown, bankers. Below them were usually only lawyers, actors, members of Congress, and polltakers.

We're trying to sort out how we should behave as this digital news decade begins. There's no doubt we love the choice. At the same time, we've gotten beyond the gee-whiz stage of childhood fascination with the wonders of infinite Internet distribution and universal, time-shifted, place-shifted news ubiquity. Now we're into the time of gawky reassessment: what's good about all this stuff, what's not so good, and how do we explain this to each other, our kids and our parents. Those are global questions we'll be wrestling with for years.

Meanwhile, let's move back to the gates that have burst open.

If it now seems like a free-for-all, let's not forget that scale and size still mean something in Web news. So let's go directly to where size matters. Let's move on to the biggest news media in the world—on both sides of the pond—and see the plans they are laying for our news future.

2

The Digital Dozen Will Dominate

Telling an immigration story had never occurred to me. But when I read an article in *The New York Times* about nineteen immigrants who had died in an abandoned refrigerator trailer in Victoria, Texas, I just saw the images the authors were describing. I saw trains, people walking on top of the trains and a green jungle world.—**CARY JOJI FUKUNAGA, filmmaker**

It's not the size of the dog in the fight, it's the size of the fight in the dog.—**MARK TWAIN, humorist**

David Pogue strides on the stage in Monterey. His audience: a couple of hundred thinkers, artists, futurists, and assorted intellectuals assembled for the "Entertainment Gathering." He's got about eighteen minutes to talk. *The New York Times*'s highest-profile personal tech writer doesn't start by talking, though. He sidles over to the piano and plays a little ditty about the iPhone. Then he talks, artfully using minimal PowerPoint, and draws on that handy little iPhone in his pocket.

A little song. A little dance. A little hot digital gadget in your pants.

David Pogue—"He's the whole package—talent, energy, wit," says the *Times'* Jon Landsman, who ran online news operations until he became Culture Editor in September last year, "is the kind of journalist media companies now love to employ."

Pogue is a journalist. He started writing for *MacWorld*, then IDG Books, and found himself in the midst of the For Dummies phenomenon, writing seven of those books. Then, in 2000, the *Times* snapped him up.

At forty-six, and, yes, a guy with musical theater talents, David Pogue is a one-man media machine. You can find his Thursday column on the front page of the business section of the print *Times* or online. His "Pogue's Posts" is one of the *Times*'s most popular blogs. His *Times* videos are self-described as "silly" and have a huge following as well. You can catch his appearances on CNBC and CBS or his Discovery cable series, *It's All Geek to Me*. He has followed up the For Dummies experience with his own Missing Manual series, making the most of Apple's minimal documentation by writing great books that answer common-sense usage questions on Macs, iPhones, and iPods.

Pogue is hard to miss on Twitter as well. He tweets regularly and has several hundred thousand followers.

David Carr, a *Times* colleague of Pogue's, is an inkstained wretch. He grew, as I did, out of the alternative press. He has written for and edited newspapers on newsprint for as long as he can remember. Today, though, as a *Times*man, his work schedule changes greatly from month to month.

He writes columns, to be sure. His Monday media column on the business front page is well read. He blogs regularly, on his own davidcarr.org blog and for the *Times*. His *Times* blog posts have ranged widely, focusing on politics, in The Caucus blog, and on the Oscars. He has branched out further, doing video interviews for the *Times*.

Writing. Editing. Reporting. Blogging. Video. And you'd never mistake Carr for someone with a musical theater background.

David Carr and David Pogue have both gone multimedia and multiplatform. Though in the vanguard, they are far from alone, being joined weekly by journalists of all kinds who are making their way in this new medium. We'll return to individual journalists and how the new Newsonomics is defining a new skill set for them, in chapter 11, "For Journalists' Jobs, It's Back to the Future."

Here, though, let's look at how big media companies are learning to harness the reach of these emerging journalistic celebrities and their wide-ranging output.

The New York Times is arguably the best-known news brand on the planet, but as it approaches its 55,000th daily edition, we still think of it as a newspaper company. You can hardly think of the *Times* without thinking of that famous masthead on newsprint. Though most assuredly it still draws more than 85 percent of its revenues from print, it is becoming a digital brand, pulling in more than 20 million "unique visitors" a month online.

In becoming a digital brand, it is harnessing the talents of its David Pogues and David Carrs—and Tom Friedmans and Paul Krugmans and Tara Parker-Popes and more. It is becoming, slowly, painfully, a multimedia company delivering its "content" in print, on desktops and laptops, on iPhones and BlackBerries, on car displays and gas station screens, and via cable TV. That's what the trade calls being "multiplatform," meaning delivering news to consumers wherever, whenever, and however they want it.

The revolution to re-create the New York Times Company and news products is in its infancy. As it reaches out, though, to areas formerly the province of broadcasters, cablecasters, Web portals, and even wire services, it helps us paint the picture of Newsonomics Law No. 2: The Digital Dozen Will Dominate. I call these global-reaching companies the Digital Dozen, though I include a few more than twelve companies among those contending to dominate the news business.

While we write and think of great news change, and great decimation of journalist workforces, let's remember that devastation is *mainly* on the local and regional level. Nationally and globally oriented companies, while struggling themselves with the transformation, see greater opportunity.

These are companies you've all heard about it—and will be hearing a lot more about. Their relative position in the news world is better than it was a few years ago. Even if they can manage to tread water—and most are doing more than that—they stand out, as local and regional companies shrink rapidly.

These Digital Dozen companies leverage one of the original Web truisms: Produce once, distribute many. In the old world of newspapers, for instance, each new copy had an incremental cost; adding more pages for advertising likewise cost more money in newsprint and ink. On the Internet, though, the cost of more is negligible, as digital production and distribution make up maybe 5–10 percent of costs. In the old analog world, newspaper publishers and broadcasters saw as much or more as a quarter of their expenses devoted to production and distribution.

The Digital Dozen then have the capability to reach far more customers than other news media, as our math shows us in "Newsonomics 101: The Digital Dozen Multiplier," below.

NEWSONOMICS 101: The Digital Dozen Multiplier . . . and the Rise in Content Unit Value

So let's see what kind of multiplier effect the members of the Digital Dozen get.

Take David Pogue's work.

If a Pogue piece of writing—let's call it a story or a post—fits on one page, and a reader goes to that page, that's a page view. Let's say that there are three ads on that page, a good average. Let's say each ad fetches $12 for each one thousand readers ($12 CPM), which should be low for tech content, but let's be conservative. "CPM" is industry jargon for cost per thousand, meaning *The New York Times* could charge an advertiser—say Best Buy—$12 for every one thousand people who view that page.

So those three ads would yield the *Times* $36 per page for every one thousand viewers.

Pogue, working for a Digital Dozen company, gets huge exposure, on the Web site, on phones, on TV, and through conferences. So let's say he generates 2 million page views a month, a fair estimate. His blog can generate half that number or more and his weekly column is highly read, so that number should be conservative.

At 2 million page views—three ads per page—that's $72,000. Not bad.

Now let's look at a tech writer for, say, the *Chicago Tribune* or *The Miami Herald*.

She or he may offer a column just as good as Pogue's, but that

(*continued*)

---

column gets far less exposure. Yes, anyone can get to the column via the Web, but the reach of the Digital Dozen's marketing and distribution relationships probably mean that the *Tribune* or *Herald* columnist reaches maybe a tenth of Pogue's—maybe, generously, 200,000 page views a month.

Though it is tech content, the *Tribune* and *Herald* don't quite carry the cachet of the *Times*, so the CPM is probably a bit lower. Let's say $8 CPM. Three ads per page.

At 200,000 page views—three ads per page—that's $4,800 a month. Not terrible, but a far cry from the $72,000 at the *Times*.

The Web business is pyramidal. Those at the top—and here it is the Digital Dozen with their global reach and marketing power—stand to take in the greatest share of revenues. They can use that money to buy and retain the best talent, generating more page views, justifying more promotion, and increasing ad revenues over time.

It could well be that going forward, media companies will be thinking in terms of content units—as odious a term as that may sound to traditional journalists. Of course, some news stories, some video clips, and some podcasts are much more valuable than others, and here, of course, the Digital Dozen have a huge distribution and promotional advantage.

On the Internet, each unit of content may be demarcated separately, with a unique identifier, a Content SKU, perhaps, just like the bar codes we see on cookie and cracker packages we buy at the market. Then as the content unit traipses its way around the digital universe, *often with ad attached*, its monetary value will be a lot to easier to track—and reap.

It's as if we're living in the aftermath of a journalistic Big Bang, still picking up the pieces of Internet dislocation—the dismemberment of the standard news business model—and learning to label them.

Why?

For starters, they are nationally and increasingly globally oriented in their coverage.

Their potential audience? Some chunk of the 900 million English-speaking people in the world, and we won't even get into multilingual or translation-on-the-fly media. So the Digital Dozen can produce a single story or single video or a single blog post and let it fly globally, connected of course to advertising. Why settle for a few hundred thousand or a few million readers in print or viewers at 6:00 P.M. when your news and advertising can traverse borders, oceans, and media habits, bringing your company far greater reach and revenue streams than you ever imagined.

Among the Digital Dozen we find newspaper companies, some broadcasters, some cablecasters, and some wires. Here we're talking about *news-producing* companies, not just those who smartly aggregate, as we'll delve into in Law No. 5.

Though all these media have differing legacy roots, their quests are converging as they seek to become winners at the emerging big business of multiplatform, multimedia global journalism. (See "Newsonomics 101: 'Papers' Beyond Words and Still Photos," below.)

NEWSONOMICS 101: "Papers" Beyond Words and Still Photos

Consider the name: the Wall Street Journal Video Network. The paper that until quite recently thought that still photographs were a bit too modern for its pages is now running its own video network.

The Web moves things at light speed, and the *Journal*'s reinvention is part of that. The WSJ Video Network leverages, smartly, the various Dow Jones properties (*WSJ*, Marketwatch, *Barron's*, and more). Every day it offers lots of news videos, though they tend to be the talking head–interview format popular on business news shows.

(continued)

News videos, especially around business content, fetch among the highest ad rates news companies can capture online.

That's why many *newspaper* companies are trying to get the knack of video.

The *Journal*'s main competitor, *The New York Times*, has gotten religion, too. Its staff of about a dozen and a half in "videography" produce—and help print staffers produce—more than twenty-five news video segments a week, ranging from Iraqi war coverage to Mark Bittman's cooking tips.

At the *Times* and at papers like *The Washington Post*, which has trained more than a quarter of its staff in video, it's very much a work in progress.

"It's a misguided notion that modern journalists have to have equal skills at Flash, video, audio," says the *Times*'s Jonathan Landman, who spent four years heading online at the *Times*. Rather, the *Times* is looking for the most interested staffers and building on those interests, believing that specialization, just as in basic reporting, will prove to be the better model. "We train people in a way that makes sense."

Newspapers are doing that from Philadelphia (the online *Nightly Business Show*) to Los Angeles (film reviews). In addition, the AP Online Video Network is trying to find a formula to share and syndicate news videos produced by its member newspapers.

Newspaper and broadcaster potential tie-ups are worth watching here. *The New York Times* is moving forward in its partnership with NBC. It started as a fairly straightforward video and text swap and is now becoming more nuanced. NBC is actually using some *Times*-produced video, in cases where the *Times* reporters have gotten to stories NBC journalists haven't. In addition, NBC is producing news shows around *Times* correspondents.

Though we think of their brands by their legacy roots—television, newspaper, radio—by 2015, I think the winners will all be known to us as big news brands associated strongly with all forms of taking in the news—reading, viewing, and listening.

They are all in the throes of big change as well, and are heavily applying most of the Newsonomics Laws we discuss here. They are all pruning their operations here and there as well, in preparation for the battles ahead. In a time of great stress, they are gingerly dismantling their old businesses, while engineering new ones on the fly.

It's true that the Digital Dozen companies have their own challenges.

Consider the travails of *The New York Times*. The *Times* has the most popular news-industry-owned news site on the Web and has created one of the most popular news applications for the iPhone. One day last April it won five Pulitzer Prizes. The next day, it suffered the indignity of announcing the biggest quarterly loss in its history—$74 million.

In a nutshell, those extremes show the challenges—top-of-the-industry achievement contrasted with poor financial performance—all these companies face.

Yet for the *Times* and the rest of the Digital Dozen, the opportunities are huge.

The Newsonomics of the Digital Dozen is impressive. You can take the same story or post or video (see "Newsonomics 101: The Digital Dozen Multiplier," page 25) and make ten times the revenue on it—if you get the business right.

Consider that what was once separate has now come together:

- In Nielsen's top 20 rankings of U.S. news Web sites, we see newspaper companies, cablecasters, broadcasters, and even aggregators, all competing head to head. The cablecasters command three of the six highest online news audiences in the United States (Fox, MSNBC, CNN).
- The pond isn't what it used to be. The U.S. news-reading market used to be wholly served by U.S. news companies; likewise, the United Kingdom was a domestic-only market. The Internet, though, has quickly turned the Atlantic Ocean into a mere puddle as online-news readers find they can cross the ocean with a few clicks of a mouse. Now, major U.K. media are making new efforts to transform those largely organically grown U.S. audiences into well-monetized markets, while the *Times* and *The Wall Street Journal* try to figure how to do likewise in Europe.

- Remember the classic *New Yorker* cartoon, "On the Internet, no one knows you're a dog." Well, on the Internet, legacy roots may show, but readers and viewers don't really care if you are a newspaper, a wire, or a TV company. They want stories. They want videos. They want audio. That's leading to a great convergence of formerly disparate media.
- Who won a Peabody, the highest award in *broadcast journalism* last year? *The New York Times*, founded in 1851.
- Who started a text wire last year? CNN, once synonymous with cable TV.

Who's in the Digital Dozen?

Let's start with newspaper-based companies like *The New York Times*. It is right up there, in its position as the leading news-owned site on the Web.

In the United States, there are only two other nationally oriented daily newspapers. First and foremost is *The Wall Street Journal*. Since Rupert Murdoch's News Corporation bought it at the end of 2006, it now competes more directly with the *Times* for advertisers. News Corp.'s holdings—and resources—go well beyond Dow Jones, *The Wall Street Journal*'s parent company, of course. They include newspapers on three continents (North America, Europe, Australia), as well as many non-newspaper businesses.

USA Today, the often-dismissed flagship newspaper of the Gannett Company, can't be overlooked, with its print circulation first in the United States and with the second-largest newspaper company in the world behind it. Then there is *The Washington Post*. Though it derives most of its business out of the prosperous D.C.-area audience, its digital reach is truly global, with more than 70 percent of its nonprint customers coming from around the country and the globe.

We can't stop at the Atlantic Ocean, though. *The Guardian*, *The Telegraph* (see "Q & A: Chris Lloyd," page 40) and Times Online—three venerable United Kingdom brands—are each making strong inroads in the United States. Each also is experimenting with video, podcasts, and blogging of all kinds.

Next, there are the broadcasters. The Big Three in the United States—NBC, ABC, and CBS—all are moving well beyond daily, scheduled television programming. (See "Newsonomics 101: The Couric/Palin Web Primer," page 20.) NBC is the company to watch here. Its move with MSNBC, NBC, CNBC, and NBC Local—combined and separately—shows that it is learning to synergize its programming and its brands. Its NBC Local unit, newly reorganized in 2008, is trying to make the network's twelve big-city TV station Web sites more newspaper-like, offering all kinds of news, info—and ads.

CBS is figuring out how to translate *The Early Show*, *The Evening News*, and *Face the Nation* to the Web. The network is trying to teach itself new tricks with its $1.8 billion purchase of online business Internet pioneer CNET in 2008.

On ABC you can catch well-ordered segments of its *Nightly News* and George Stephanopolous's weekly talk show—one among what humorist Calvin Trillin delightfully calls the "Sabbath gasbag" programs—rather than trying to remember to TiVo it. The full-featured ABCNews site can look remarkably newspaper-like, as it offers blog compilations like "Political Punch" and "Campus Chatter."

Again, on the other side of the pond, let's not forget the BBC. Funded by TV license fees and commercial free in the United Kingdom, it has targeted the United States for its programming—and here it can sell ads.

Then there are the cablecasters. In addition to resurgent MSNBC, CNN and Fox News lay claim to Digital Dozen membership.

CNN, the largest cable news network, emerged as the leading news source in the 2008 elections, as broadcasters peeled back and cablecasters filled the void, thereby picking up large audiences. CNN now has more than 3,800 employees, about the same as the ubiquitous wire services, the Associated Press and Reuters. In fact, in December 2008, it announced that it would launch a new wire service. CNN, which had first used a fair amount of wire service content, had grown big and hungry enough to compete against the wires.

CNN's sometime-kissing-cousin is Time Inc.; both operations are owned by Time Warner. Time Inc.'s *Fortune* has been folded into CNNMoney, while *Time* struggles to redefine itself. With a portfolio of leading magazine brands—*People, Entertainment Weekly, Sunset, Southern Living*—Time Inc. may become a Digital Dozen player in its own right.

Fox News, the brainchild of News Corporation ace Roger Ailes, has proven a tough competitor to CNN. It has now added a business news channel. Fox, like CNN, sees the appeal of user-generated content. Its U Report, like CNN's iReport, is set to gather, assemble, and make money of user contributions around the globe.

Of course, the Associated Press and Reuters are both fighting back against CNN's venture into their territory. Originally text-only services—born in the era of "miracle" telegraph lines—they are becoming multimedia producers, with much investment in video production as well. Though they supply lots of content to other media, they are both becoming part of the exclusive Digital Dozen group. Reuters has the advantage of having recently been merged into information-industry giant Thomson Reuters, giving it still greater reach and resources.

Reuters's strategy is twofold, providing its news wire to major media throughout the world, while building its own Web site and separate identity. It doesn't just want to be a supplier to the Digital Dozen; it wants to be one of them.

AP's future is murkier. As a nonprofit cooperative, owned by U.S. newspaper companies, it is by nature a supplier of news. Yet its members—those local dailies looking for every way to cut costs—have been rebelling at its prices and looking for alternatives. Some are even looking to CNN as an alternative. So AP, which generates about 75 percent of its revenue from sources other than local newspapers, may well decide it needs to take an independent turn in order to remain a major player. (See "Q & A: Jim Kennedy," page 97.)

In talking about the Digital Dozen, we can't forget an audio player, National Public Radio. NPR's traditional audience continues to grow. About 27.5 million people listen to NPR each week, averaging 4.5 hours per week, a listenership that has grown at almost a 10 percent clip. That's a huge number, and one that if better translated to the Internet could make NPR a big player.

Not subject to the vagaries of advertising, and supported increasingly by foundation funding, NPR has been able to ramp up both on-air and Internet programming, relaunching NPR.org last summer. Importantly, it makes use of Americans' multitasking addictions; there's nothing easier to listen to than time-shifted, in-the-background audio when working, browsing, or e-mailing. With the late 2008 addition of New York Times Digital veteran Vivian Schiller as CEO, it intends to be one of the Digital Dozen.

Finally, there are a couple of other big financial news and information providers. Business news is the most lucrative business on the Web, as we'll explore in Law No. 8, garnering the highest advertising rates. When money changes hands, readers are more willing to pay for news that informs their decisions.

So here, add in *Financial Times*, the U.K. equivalent of *The Wall Street Journal*, and the only news company other than the *Journal* to have successfully charged its readers for online access.

Then, consider Bloomberg, the once-upstart business built on providing proprietary terminals to companies keen on getting up-to-the-second business news and data. It has subsequently given birth to a whole empire of TV, radio, and online sites. Take a look into the Bloomberg newsroom where reporters sit at terminals typing away at stories to be transmitted instantly around the globe and then twirl to smile for the TV camera as they are interviewed live on cable.

Yes, I know, I've listed sixteen parent companies, so let's call it an editor's dozen. I do expect that the group will be about an even dozen as mergers and consolidation set in, in the years ahead.

Digital Dozen brands are much recognized by their stars. Paging Dr. Sanjay Gupta. CNN matches the *Times*'s high-profile talents with its Guptas, Coopers, Kings, Amanpours, and Zakarias. Fox's O'Reillys, Hannitys, and Becks go up against MSNBC's Matthewses, Olbermanns, and Maddows. ABC lines up its Tappers, McFaddens, and Bashirs versus NBC's Williamses, Todds, and Gregorys versus NPR's Wertheimers, Elvings, and Conans.

These names draw in huge audiences. Personalities have long fronted the news, from TV anchors to newspaper columnists. Today, they still are news people, but they are also front men and women, promoters and digital barkers, using everything from tweeting to traveling around the world to sell the goods.

If personalities draw the audiences in, it is the depth and breadth of the hundreds and thousands of journalists working alongside the bigger names that give the news brands their resonance in our lives. Increasingly, these journalists are using multimedia—with their allure of fulfilling pictures, voices, and words—to deliver the news.

We can look at the Digital Dozen through the prism of multimedia—and multitasking. It's not unusual for reporters to do multimedia turns on the same story, on the same day. Bloomberg is ahead of the game in its relentless multitasking. A reporter is expected to write a four-hundred-word wire story—for Bloomberg, being first is the first order of business. Then, she'll "write through" the story several times, updating it as she completes interviews. She may do some audio for Bloomberg's radio station or be interviewed for its podcasts or pop up on Bloomberg TV.

Multimedia sometimes means just being interviewed on other media. *New York Times* and *Wall Street Journal* reporters are often called on for story-based interviews on NPR. *Washington Post* columnists are a hot commodity for cable talkfests.

It's a media circus centered on multiplatform (print, TV, radio, Web) and cross promotion. It's an endless 24/7 game that is always being played or planned. The currency: building the brand awareness, bringing more people—audience—to your shop rather than the other guy's. The more audience, the more advertising you can sell, and that pays the bills.

The Internet has proven to be the great meeting ground for all these big news companies of diverse legacies. For newspaper companies, the video revolution began in fits and starts in the late nineties. We saw experiments here and there, as the print-based companies fumbled to produce their own video segments or partnered with broadcasters.

Of course, that was an era in which we as consumers could hardly watch video online.

Flash forward, and a majority of us have broadband connections and have gotten used to the delights of YouTube video and watching news segments online whenever we want.

So *The Washington Post* has now trained more than a quarter of its newsroom on producing video. *The New York Times* creates more than 100 segments a month (see "Newsonomics 101: 'Papers' Beyond Words and Still Photos," page 27). Telegraph TV, a focal point of the London-based site, is a top source for Britons.

For broadcasters and cablecasters, it's been the inverse challenge: written words. CNN's on-air reporters are now writing columns for the Web site.

Increasingly, we as consumers expect our news sites to give us the best of the best. Sometimes that is video, sometimes audio, sometimes text, often all three nested together. Look at the sites of the Digital Dozen today, and their presentation—what they emphasize—displays their roots. The TV people are heavy in visuals, the print people heavy in text. That won't last, as our digital news decade takes hold.

With multimedia increasingly expected by us readers, the price of admission for the Digital Dozen is near-absolute 24/7 timeliness.

We're well past the era (well, the late nineties) when editors and producers hemmed and hawed about whether to "hold" a story for air or print. You get the news now; you publish it on the Web.

On a Saturday in April 2009, the word of Mexico's swine flu "potential pandemic" swept through the news day. Sure, AP and Reuters were right on the story, but so were—immediately—*The Washington Post*, *Time* magazine, the Huffington Post, Al-Jazeera, and *The Guardian*, among hundreds of media outlets.

You can't believe the sturm und drang that newsrooms of all kinds have gone through in the past decade, as reorganizations—put the print and Web people together, separate, together!—drove journalists nuts. Those reorganizations are still in process, but Web-first journalism, and increasingly, Web-only, is becoming the rule, not the exception.

Personality. Multimedia. Timeliness. Next up: The ability to transcend national roots will be a test for the Digital Dozen.

We're now in the first stage of companies truly becoming global.

For major U.K. media, like the BBC, *Guardian*, and *Telegraph*, about a third of their unique visitors online are found in the United States. Yet that audience contributes less than 5 percent of those companies' revenues. Similarly, *The New York Times* finds one-third of its audience outside the United States, but non-U.S. revenues have been stuck at 4 percent.

Those are big opportunities, and the Digital Dozen winners will seize on them as they solve two problems. One is a sales problem:

Which staff do you use to establish new relationships with significant ad buyers? How do you use the targeting ad technologies of the day—wherever readers are—to match up all audiences smartly with premium advertising?

Neither is a trivial pursuit, but both will be solved.

We see greater attention to developing new news products that overseas audiences may see as their own. Last year, *The Wall Street Journal* strengthened its European presence, planning new local sections for Europe on WSJ.com to create a "more regionally relevant experience for readers." *The New York Times* launched a new global edition, replacing the Europe-based *International Herald Tribune*'s Web site. The goals: leverage the increasingly sophisticated *Times* platforms for video, multimedia, and ad targeting. The new edition is the first major attempt to take the *Times* brand truly global. *The Guardian* launched its own U.S. edition in 2007, complete with a five-person D.C. bureau.

There's another way that the Digital Dozen take advantage of their reach, mating with each other and with major suppliers of news in more distant lands. *The New York Times* and NBC have partnered: The *Times* gets video; NBC gets *Times* writers and columnists on air—and the precious "text" that broadcast companies need online. Such day-to-day partnerships are essential; they extend resources at fairly low cost.

It's the big story, though, that can tell more about the value of news interconnections.

Take the audacious Mumbai terror attack of 2008. India's New York was under siege. In the chaos of multiple-target attacks, it was a live story with great drama. If you turned to CNN, you saw some CNN anchors, but mainly you saw direct feeds from IBN, one of India's leading broadcasters. If you turned to MSNBC, you got NDTV, another leading company. In fact, NDTV is one of the leaders globally in having viewers contribute to its programs through social networking, an extension that paid big dividends during the terror attacks. Both partnerships, already in place before the big news, made CNN and MSNBC must-watch outlets on that story. Such partnerships, of course, existed in the old world of news. Now, though, they are being newly knit together. It's like the kind of code sharing that airlines long ago figured out as an efficiency, now applied to news.

The news product is one thing, but sales are another, and probably more important.

Here companies with longer and better developed overseas audiences and sales channels have an advantage. *The Financial Times* has developed a small niche audience—and sales force—in the United States. Similarly, CNN, conceived as a global-facing company and now offering a number of global versions of itself, has a head start over other media trying to master the new international language of commerce.

One other factor may separate the winners from the losers. That factor seems less obvious, but is hugely important as advertising shifts away from newspapers, magazines, and broadcast TV largely to Web-based marketing, as we'll see in Law No. 4. Those news operations that are part of bigger, diversified companies have an advantage.

Take the competition between *The New York Times* and *The Wall Street Journal*. They are two New York–based daily newspaper companies, both now growing into multimedia, multiplatform companies and both top members of the Digital Dozen.

They used to be two different creatures. The *Times* focused on being the nation's and New York's general interest source; the *Journal* was the nation's business paper.

Their businesses grew closer over the years, as the Internet blurred lines and as advertisers started figuring out the significant overlap between their two audiences.

The battle was really joined, though, when Rupert Murdoch's News Corporation bought Dow Jones & Co. and the *Journal* in December 2007 and declared its intention to bury the *Times*. Since then, the news operations have competed directly, both beefing up business and tech reporting and going after the same luxury advertisers. The *Journal* has also added more general news and sports news—and in the process become more *Times*-like.

There's one big corporate difference between the two companies. *The New York Times* is almost wholly dependent on the news business. Its nonnews Internet businesses contribute less than 5 percent of its revenues.

The *Journal*, on the other hand, is part of the bigger, diversified News Corporation. Not only does News Corp. own the biggest news company in the world, with operations in the United Kingdom, Australia and the United States, but that company is just a division of News Corp. In fact, the News Corp. News Division is responsible for just about 20 percent of News Corp. revenues. The rest: diversified satellite, cable, and film businesses, including 20th Century–Fox. So, in a given year, News Corp. can make up for subpar *Journal* ad performance with a box office–busting Ben Stiller movie.

Similarly, CNN gains an advantage by being part of big, diverse Time Warner, and it balances its ad revenue with direct cable fees paid by distributors. MNSBC is part of NBC, which is owned by General Electric. ABC is part of Disney. Reuters News is but a small part, about 10 percent, of Thomson Reuters.

Bloomberg? It's a stand-alone, but has a rich parent. While it has made many moves entering radio, TV, and the free Web markets, it still gets 90 percent of its revenues from use of those Bloomberg machines, situated in financial, corporate, public relations, and journalism offices worldwide. The Washington Post Company, struggling with its newspapers and *Newsweek*, takes in more than 50 percent of its revenue from its Kaplan Education business these days.

Most vulnerable of the newspaper-based companies are those wholly or mostly dependent on printed news, such as *The New York Times*, *The Telegraph*, and maybe even *The Guardian*, though its nonprofit Scott Trust funding provides a buffer of another kind. The Associated Press, too, is wholly dependent on news, though a bit cushioned by licensing it to nonnews companies.

NPR? Its membership model could provide substantial and growing support or it could doom it to being a minor player.

As we survey this key question of ownership and deep pockets, it's essential to look at that morphing word: media.

In this book I'm distinguishing between the news business and media. Think back to just thirty years ago. Journalism, news, and media were fairly synonymous. Media meant the *Times*, the *Post*, your local daily, and CBS News, ABC News, and NBC News.

Now we define media much more broadly.

There are those conglomerates—the News Corps, Disneys, Time Warners, General Electrics—that include news in their portfolios. They are media companies (other than GE) whose main business is entertainment. Then there are the pipes companies who now fancy themselves as media companies, though they are really distributors for lots of content and communication. Think Comcast, ATT, and Verizon.

Then, there are lots of media companies whose activities touch the news. Think Google, Amazon, and Yahoo.

Bottom line: Far fewer companies of any size now see news as their main business. We can argue that the financial security provided by a larger company is a good thing for news producers and consumers. Or we can argue we're losing our bearings completely, as "news" gets subsumed into the larger world of business, where the profit motive is the main motivator and "public service" seems a philanthropic thing to do—if you can afford it.

If size and scale matter just to get into the Digital Dozen club, they'll matter as much to stay in it and prosper.

Of course, we don't know who may join the Digital Dozen, or who might drop out. Maybe smaller news organizations will grow great. More likely, we'll see more alliances between the Digital Dozen and emerging news producers.

Reuters's recent agreement with the fast-rising Politico Web site is a good example of the aggregation we'll explore in Law No. 5. Reuters gets more content into its worldwide distribution system, and Politico gets more audience and brand awareness. (In turn, Politico has set up its own Politico Network, an agreement with local news sites to share political news content and advertising.) In all of these agreements, the parties share revenue and get more traffic.

CNN needed to get more local, so it entered into an agreement with local broadcast stations and reaps the benefit of extra traffic and some content exchange.

The future holds the likelihood of lots of similar relationships. Already we see new news brands like start-up GlobalPost (discussed later, in chapter 8) working with the BBC and CBS. We can see the potential of the Public Broadcasting System's *NewsHour* going in that direction online. PBS finally launched its own contemporary site last year. As PBS gets its arms around the digital future, it can better harness such fare as Charlie Rose's interviews. On the Web, they become long-form, segmented video, a now-valuable archive for PBS and for partners.

What we're seeing is really an emerging ecosystem in birth. Maybe we had best look at the system as a new media family tree, with lots of big brothers, little sisters, and more cousins than we can count.

It's very early in the Digital Dozen competition. Distribution and advertising technologies have just gotten to a point where sophisticated, multination, multimedia, multiplatform plays can be tested. The recession slowed down the players a bit, as they prudently preserved their firepower to fight another day.

Now, that day is arriving. Each member of the Digital Dozen will follow its own strategy.

Within those strategies we will see all the principles of Newsonomics. Already we see the head-to-head competition for lucrative niche readers, in business, technology, health, and travel. Already we see a rush to perfect the best mobile applications for smartphones. Already we see major pushes to sign up the best talent of the day, whether from a competitor or from the top end of the blogosphere. Already we see a push to incorporate the journalism-friendly tools of blogging and social networking deeply into their enterprises. Already we see the doubling down on investment in technology to harness its abilities to save labor and please consumers.

What we don't see is the Digital Dozen putting a major effort into getting local. That's an expensive proposition, with smaller payoff for them. Which brings us to the flip side of the global arena in which the Digital Dozen will dominate. It's the local arena in which we're seeing the most profound and fastest changes.

Q & A: Chris Lloyd

Chris Lloyd is an assistant managing editor for the London-based Telegraph. *He has won lots of recognition for leading one of the first (2006) major multimedia newsroom restructurings, a redo that brought content creation together, physically and organizationally. The move served as a foundation for growing the digital business, enabling ahead-of-the-industry Web-first and video content and reader interaction. Telegraph TV is one of the main news video players in the U.K. market, and the site overall counts a third of its readers in the United States.*

Q: You were an early leader in newsroom transformation and video. What news event confirmed to you, early on, that all the work you'd done had gotten you ready to excel at a big story?

A: The foiled Heathrow airport terror attack in the summer of 2006 was probably the first story that confirmed we were heading in the right direction. It was a story that moved very quickly throughout the day, and it benefited from video and audio coverage as well as text. Continuously updating the Web site as the story unfolded was crucial, as so many people were potentially affected through flight cancellations, etc. It was the first event where we sent a reporter with camera and produced video footage to supplement the online copy.

Q: Do you think Telegraph.co.uk customers now see *Telegraph* as more than a newspaper company? What's the kind of reaction you've gotten from them?

A: I think it takes a long time to change perceptions, but we are gradually getting there. Our commercial customers (ad agencies and clients) are certainly aware that we are much more than a newspaper these days. As for our readers, I think this will take longer, but we take a lot of care to tell them about the additional content available to them online.

Q: Ten years from now, do you think there'll be much of a difference in the type of news content *Telegraph* produces and a news broadcaster produces?

A: I think we will continue to provide a much broader depth and breadth of content than traditional news broadcasters, who will typically concentrate on a narrower range of news stories. We will

3

Local: Remap and Reload

I read about eight newspapers in a day. When I'm in a town with only one newspaper, I read it eight times. —**WILL ROGERS**

We're not trying to replace the daily newspaper.—**ANDREW DONAHUE,** editor of the *Voice of San Diego*

First thing in the morning, Joel Kramer checks in on the news, by habit, reading the papers first of course, the *Star-Tribune* and *The New York Times*—and his own online news Web site, MinnPost.

Then he's off to new workweeks of 50–60 hours, spending three-quarters of that time talking to would-be sponsors, donors and foundations. It's not a next career step he'd planned, and even he seems surprised that it is one he has taken.

At sixty-one, Joel Kramer is editor, publisher, chief fund-raiser, angel in chief, and public face of MinnPost. You couldn't ask for someone with better journalism bona fides to head the Twin Cities start-up news site. Kramer had retired as publisher of the *Star-Tribune,* the once-dominant daily of the Minneapolis–Saint Paul metro area. He'd come to Minneapolis to become editor of the paper in 1983—a year that now seems light-years away to him in journalism time. He became publisher in 1992 and retired in 1997 when the McClatchy Company bought the paper from its longtime family owner, the Cowles family. He stayed busy, heading a think tank, Growth & Justice.

It wasn't the siren call of a newspaper that called him back; it was an alarm bell instead. Like most readers of the *Star-Tribune* and the *Pioneer Press*, he watched in amazement as byline after byline disappeared from the papers as they shrank, not only in staff but in height, width, weight, and—most important—news. So he decided to put his journalism hat back on, but this time with a twist.

He convinced his wife Laurie that it was worth putting some of their own money into a new journalism venture, and he persuaded three other local families as well. They collectively put up $850,000, and MinnPost was conceived in December 2007.

MinnPost has seen explosive growth, attracting a half million "unique visitors" a month, who look at a couple of million pages.

On its pages: Dozens of those familiar faces and bylines that the *Star-Tribune* and the *Pioneer Press* had jettisoned in buyouts and layoffs.

MinnPost hit the market at the right time and not only in its ability to pick up high-value labor on the cheap. It walked into an intense Minnesota political year, with the Al Franken–Norm Coleman Senate battle playing out for an eternity. Increasingly, it is trying to carve out time to do investigative work, a field that in and of itself is changing greatly, as we see in "Newsonomics 101: New Kennels for the Watchdogs," page 67.

Good fortune or not, it's in the MinnPost business model that we glimpse the local online future.

MinnPost is a small operation, supporting about a dozen people at workmanlike Twin Cities middle-class wages. Those people behind the familiar bylines? They're happy to work for a real journalistic outfit again, and one that is growing, but some are only getting paid about $1,000 a month, compared to the $5,000 a month they were used to at the dailies. (See "Newsonomics 101: Start-up Business Models," page 60.)

Meanwhile, the two dailies that have freed up all those contributors for MinnPost?

They are poster children for the woes of the local daily press.

The *Star Tribune*, or the *Strib* as we called it, has just emerged from bankruptcy, after new owners overpaid for the paper in 2007.

The *Pioneer Press*, one of my alma maters, is owned by MediaNews, a company itself that has skirted on the edge of financial default.

Both are shadows of their former selves. The *Strib*, once home to 425 in its newsroom, is down to about 275. The *Pioneer Press* is way down to 120 from a peak of about 225 when I served there as managing editor in the mid-nineties.

What happened?

Those two papers and the well-educated, well-informed Twin Cities metro area are emblematic of the press devastation we've witnessed in cities across America. While the Digital Dozen trimmed their sails in the recession, it's the local press that has seen huge holes blown directly in their ships. While we've never seen such robust discussions of national or universal topics like the health care meltdown, green industrial initiatives, charter school experience and policy, and even the future of news, we've never seen such constricting of local news. For truly local news, our supply lines are being cut.

Over the years, the ravages of Internet competition had damaged the local press more than the national, and then the recession came along, just as a fierce storm whacks off the limbs of weakened trees.

That's a big problem because, in the United States, most of our press has long been local. (Europe, with its less far-flung geography, has long seen greater national press readership, and that has so far made some difference in the prospects for its journalism.)

Consider that of 1,500 or so daily papers in the United States, only three are truly national—*The New York Times*, *The Wall Street Journal*, and *USA Today*. The rest are metros and city dailies. For decades, it has been those local papers that have brought half or more of the households in most cities their daily news. In most metro areas, the *Times* and the *Journal* reach no more than 5 percent of the households, and usually significantly less.

Bottom line: For most Americans, it has been their local papers that delivered the day's news. Consequently, the winnowing of the local press will have profound impacts on most of us.

It's an impact that is tough for most readers to quantify. In communities, you most often hear about the lack of coverage anecdotally. You're involved in the local service club, or around a major development controversy, or raising money for an arts organization—and there's no one to talk to at the paper, and you don't see your issue covered. And you know, though it's like fumbling in the darkness, that there is just a lot of other stuff not being covered.

There are many markers of what we're losing.

CONSIDER:

- *Local journalism has taken the brunt of the pain.* There have been at least seven local newspaper companies that have declared bankruptcy, and most others have been spending as much time with their bankers as with their businesses. Let's recall the numbers: At least 20 percent fewer stories done by at least 20 percent fewer newsroom staff. While the Digital Dozen counts their journalistic workforce in the thousands, daily newspapers have long counted them in the lower hundreds. The loss in U.S. newsroom jobs since the 2001 peak of 56,900: 12,900, or 22 percent. With about 8,000 jobs lost in the last two years, we can estimate that readers have lost tens of thousands of years of community knowledge. Disproportionately, the older, the more experienced (and most highly paid) staff is targeted for buyouts and layoffs. (See "Newsonomics 101: Newspapers C-O-O-L It," page 92.)

- *Big, sprawling regional metros have been the big losers.* In 2009, many of them, like the *San Jose Mercury News* and *The Dallas Morning News*, *The Atlanta Journal-Constitution*, and *The Miami Herald* saw circulation dips in the *teens*, after absorbing 3+ percent declines for four years. Where once these papers sent reporters all over the world and maintained bureaus from Beijing to Mexico City to Moscow, they've all cut back dramatically on far-flung coverage. If they can't see it from the top floor of their newspaper building, they probably aren't covering it.

- *The year 2009 marked the beginning of hybrid journalism.* The hundred-year-old *Christian Science Monitor* was one of the first to fold its daily print operation and go online, save for one Saturday edition. More than seven dozen daily newspapers have dropped at least a single day of the week in publishing, and many more than one. They've pushed their readers to the Web for the news. In the process, we saw the phenomenon of daily newspapers that were no longer daily. (See "Newsonomics 101: Creating the Local New Print/Online Hybrids," page 48.)

- *Some papers are giving up print entirely.* Hearst threw in the towel with its print *Post-Intelligencer*, Seattle's second largest daily, in early 2009. Newhouse closed *The Ann Arbor News* last summer. Both are part of the online-only experimentation.
- *Local broadcast companies are playing catch-up, and are now growing their online audiences and revenues at a faster rate than local newspapers.* They started several steps behind newspapers, but are following the same storyline. Now, as their on-air audiences lag and their stagnant ad revenues have gotten them labeled "mature" businesses, the local broadcasters are making their own moves. Broadcast chains, including LIN TV, Gray Television, and Meredith Broadcasting are early leaders in this area. We also see media networks like WorldNow, Internet Broadcasting, and Broadcast Interactive Media powering Web sites for many local broadcasters. The broadcasters contribute their video, some text writing, and lots of promotion. The media networks provide the technology, lots of national features (stock tickers, national news, traffic reports, health info modules, and more), and advertising sales and support. ("Newsonomics 101: Here Come the Local Broadcasters," page 64, looks at this new competitiveness.)
- *Smaller city newspapers are faring a bit better.* Yes, they've trimmed too, losing some readers and some advertising, but they are surviving better than their metro brothers. With their most intensive local focus, they're better suited to survive Internet competition, though they are now facing new competition as big dailies are trying to get "local-local."
- *News start-ups on the Web have exploded in number, in public interest and in funding potential.* From New Haven to San Diego and Seattle to Washington, D.C., if there isn't an independent online news site in your city, there will be soon.

How did such changes come about? We'll get into the profound changes in news publishing economics in our next chapter, "The Old News World Is Gone. Get Over It."

These new economics have forced a basic redefinition of local news. It's a change with a lot more impact than the Digital Dozen's, whose companies are focusing on *how* they do their journalism— more Web-first, more multimedia, more personality driven.

For local news companies, it is more basic: What do we cover and where do we cover it? Basically, the old news formulas and definitions have been thrown out the window. We're in the midst of complete reinvention.

These local journalism companies are increasingly about two things: local content production and local sales. Forget the thundering old iron printing presses, truck distribution, and big finance departments.

We're seeing two distinct kinds of operations reinventing local news.

The biggest local news companies—the newspapers—are not only reinventing, they're downsizing rapidly, and, I believe, permanently. The smaller local news companies—the start-ups—are finding innovative ways to get bigger. Big companies are getting smaller. Small companies are getting bigger. The big question: Will these two trend lines meet, and, if so, where?

NEWSONOMICS 101: Creating the Local New Print/ Online Hybrids

2009 brought us the Hybrid Age of News(papers), with a vengeance. In just one week's time in March, we heard announcements that would render the state of Michigan—the United States' eighth-largest with ten million people—far less covered.

The *Detroit Free Press* and the *News* said they would become effectively three-day-a-week "dailies," delivering to homes only on those days. Sure, they still publish something in print the other four days, but not more than thirty-two pages in one or two sections, while they urge their readers to go online for the latest news. The only places to get the skinnied version: on the news-

(continued)

---

stand, unless you live in a nursing home! That's right: nursing home residents still get seven-day delivery. That's something between charity and target marketing.

They've accelerated their own *print* demise, and they've got lots of company. More than seven dozen other dailies have cut back on days of production. The goal is clear: hang on to as much print advertising as possible, while making a transition to mainly digital business. That means pushing, shoving, cajoling, bundling, and pricing advertisers into whichever print days are left, your basic Sundays, Fridays, maybe a Wednesday or Thursday. Monday, Tuesday? Never liked those days anyway!

Outside Detroit, we saw cutbacks announced across the state in the same month. In Flint, Saginaw, and Bay City, newspapers are moving from seven-day dailies (there, the oxymoronic need to define) to three-day dailies. They also promised lots of Web-first and Web-special content.

What began in panic—newspapers cutting costs as rapidly as possible—is evolving into something of a strategy.

Here's the basic Newsonomics:

- Hold on to as much of the current print advertising as you can. Print advertising still amounts to 85 percent of the revenues of most newspaper companies. That means the print days kept are the market days—those days current advertisers prize most. Sunday often yields more than 50 percent of revenues, so that's the big day. Encourage and give encouraging pricing to advertisers to move their ads to those days, trying to minimize loss of placements even as publishing days are eliminated.
- Reduce those legacy costs quickly and dramatically. So, if papers don't publish in print, they don't have to pay pressmen to run the presses, or production people to create the pages. They don't have to move stacks of newsprint, fuel trucks, or pay delivery people. Print-and-delivery costs generally run 25 to 30 percent of a newspaper's overall costs.

(*continued*)

The basic idea is easy to see: cut costs by more than the print ad revenues you'll inevitably lose.

Short-term, this off-the-cuff strategy may work. Advertisers may be inclined to give it a try, and the cost savings are immediate. The biggest peril for publishers embarking on this strategy: as they push readers to the Web several days of the week, how many of them will drop the print habit *sooner than later*? If they do, circulation will further plummet and those print advertisers—who still pay most of the bills—will follow them online, where they pay less for advertising, a new vicious circle in the making.

As one news executive of a big company with dozens of local newspapers spread across the United States told me, "I'm not sure if these guys are ankle biters or something more." Good Silicon Valley lesson. The ankle biters can grow up quickly and develop big teeth.

I've called Newsonomics Law No. 3: Local: Remap and Reload. That's remapping in the basic way that local is being redefined. That's reloading in the sense of understanding that while one battle has plainly been lost—that of keeping the local press intact as we knew it—another is ahead. The tools and weapons to be used in this new battle require reloading. Reloading new ways of who's doing journalism—what to report, how to report it, who to report it, where they are reporting it from, and even why they are doing it.

We'll return to how all of these companies—big and small, print and broadcast—are reloading throughout the rest of the book, as we look at how they are engaging their communities, how they are using blogging, and how they are appealing to specific niche audiences.

Remap. We all used to know local. You know a city. Detroit. Fort Myers, Portland. Local's gotten all mixed up on the Web, though. We can see two big reasons for that.

The first is that the Web lets us define "local" any way we want. It's like the city is one big Google map, with those plus and minus zooms. Care about your block, neighborhood, zip? You can zero in there, courtesy of technology brought to you by aggregators like Topix, Outside In, and even Google itself. Or maybe you do care about the city itself. Or the region. Follow your mouse and take in as much or as little of the city as you wish. News, entertainment listings, family events, parks, and more.

The second is that the Internet has forced local media companies to redefine themselves. We no longer need those local editors to select stories and package news of the nonlocal world. We can go to the NYTimes.com, or MarketWatch or ESPN, among hundreds of other top sites, ourselves, thank you.

So publishers, editors, station directors, and producers are busy redefining what exactly local turf now means. For some, it means going after the citywide schools and crime and local government stories. For some, it means intensive family coverage. For others, it means hyperlocal. When they say "hyperlocal," they mean really, *really* local, or neighborhood oriented. That's proven hard to define, and harder to cover, but we'll meet some of the companies going there.

In redefining local, those directing revamped operations are trying to plot out new strategies amid the carnage of lost jobs, diminished products, and dampened spirits. They are trying to apply laws of Newsonomics—especially in the combination of the work of professional journalists and the contributions of community members and in blogging, going after niche audiences and multimedia production. The results so far: highly incomplete.

Kate Marymont is a newspaper veteran. She is considered one of Gannett's most innovative editors, and that won her the job as vice president of news for the company, the U.S.'s largest publisher of daily newspapers. Marymont is clear that plans are constantly in motion for Gannett. "Part of our evolution is thinking that not everyone can do everything. We're thinking more about specialists for print, for mobile, for digital."

Gannett owns daily papers across the United States, eighty-two of them, and the United Kingdom's third biggest chain, Newsquest. It's also got a major presence in local broadcast, with twenty-two stations owned. In addition, the company publishes *USA Today*, the largest paper by circulation in the United States.

Gannett has long been seen as the savviest operator in the business. For Wall Street, that's been a compliment. Those operating skills produced profit margins beyond 30 percent in the go-go years of the trade. For those in newsrooms, fairly or not, Gannett has been synonymous with doing *good-enough* journalism, good enough to maintain its once-strong business.

What Gannett always has had is an ability to move more centrally than its peers. While many other companies took the "local autonomy" notion as a divine law, Gannett was never shy about imposing diversity guidelines (in hiring and content), in mandating designs and story lengths, and in just being pushier than its newspaper company brethren.

Now Gannett, having seen the writing on the wall, has embarked on the biggest mandated change in the company's history. Seemingly, every month it announces a new initiative. Though many are fledgling and may seem fragmentary, overall, we're seeing a set of initiatives that are a prototype of basic remapping and reloading.

The Gannett revolution begins with its Information Centers. Announced in 2007, the centers represent nothing less than the reinvention of the local print—and broadcast—newsroom.

Its mantra embraces seven songs:

- Local, Local, Local: Here, Gannett's throwing in the towel and acknowledging that readers can get their nonlocal coverage elsewhere.
- Public Service: The aim here is coverage that makes a difference in community life. Gannett's *Free Press* won a Pulitzer Prize last year for its series on the misdeeds of former Detroit mayor Kwame Kilpatrick.
- Custom Content: That has meant new "microsites," as Gannett bought microsite technology company Ripple6. Its MomsLikeMe .net and HighSchoolSports.net sites are deployed across the country, new products I describe in chapter 8, "Itch the Niche." They target specific reader audiences, and ads for them are now sold through the Gannett Digital Media Network. In 2009 the com-

pany took its old Gannett News Service and folded it into ContentOne. The name's niftier, and here, too, Gannett's directional approach is clear: Bring all its content—print, broadcast and digital—together in one place, and then create lots of advertising-friendly niche products.

- Multimedia: Gannett's in the midst of cross-training reporters and photographers, believing that its journalists should be able to tell stories in text—and sound and moving pictures. As Kate Marymont points out, though, you have to pick and choose carefully. Some reporters can learn to deliver great video stand-ups; others can barely stand still in front of a camera.
- Data: Information Centers, of course, emphasizes "information," not news. Gannett understands that readers often just want to know what's happening, where it's happening, and how to find services in their community. "Data Central," a focus of the Gannett local sites, offers all kinds of public database material, from government official salaries to FAA bird-strike records to public school scores. The company owns Metromix, a set of entertainment sites, and is making "calendaring" a key part of its new products.
- Community Conversation: Gannett uses the Pluck social networking tools across its sites. That means lots of comments, forum discussions, citizen blog posts, and uploading of photos and videos from readers and viewers. It also means lots more blogging by Gannett reporters and columnists.
- Digital: This is Gannett's overall aspiration. Easier said than done, the company is trying to become medium agnostic, delivering to print, desktop, and mobile media.

Its Westchester property, the *Journal News*, is prototypical of Gannett's Info Center moves, embracing prep coverage, intensive blogging and changing reporter roles. (See chapter 7, "Reporters Become Bloggers.")

So what impact has all this made?

In truth, Gannett can't quite say yet, nor can many other companies. It's too early.

Print circulation continues to plummet at Gannett and all other large dailies.

Readers are coming to newspapers' local online sites, tens of millions of them across the country, but at this point they're not staying. The average local newspaper-owned Web site is lucky to see its average visitor spend more than twelve minutes per month. Compare that to the hours readers have traditionally spent with newspapers in print each week.

That's the state of things—for Gannett and its brethren. The New Local is a start.

All newspaper companies are taking pages from the same playbook, though Gannett's push is more public and more sweeping. Scripps is pushing together its local newspaper and local broadcast sites as never before. McClatchy emphasizes staff blogs. Hearst pushes the envelope of local citizen blogs.

Indeed, the roles of editors are changing in many places, as some become more community organizers than wordsmiths. At *The Hartford Courant*, a half dozen editors have been assigned to work with community members in six areas around the metro area—all to get more local news at a lower cost.

Across the country, dailies are trying out variants of the *Courant*'s current strategy. *The Washington Post* has tried it in the exurbs and suburbs and found it too expensive for the investment, so it's reloading and trying new twists on the theme.

People do want good local coverage, but it's expensive to pay professional journalists to do it. And civilians need lots of support, encouragement, and reminders. Mark Potts, who pioneered the $3 million-funded Backfence, a mid-decade approach to developing hyperlocal sites and then networking them, has blogged about the difficulties of making it all work.

"Hyperlocal is really hard. Don't kid yourself. You don't just open the doors and hit critical mass. We knew that from the jump. It takes a lot of work to build a community. Look carefully at most hyperlocal sites and see just how much posting is really being done, especially by members of the community as opposed to the sites' operators. Anybody who's run a hyperlocal site will tell you that it takes a couple of years just to get to a point where you've truly got a vibrant online community. It takes even longer to turn that into a viable business. Unfortunately, for a variety of reasons, Backfence was unable to sustain itself long enough to reach that point."

Local dailies have listened to that lesson and hope to learn from it. Their calculus: Get their remaining, if shrunken staffs, to focus only on local news, write more of it (including updates throughout the day, posted online), and engage community members to contribute "content"—covering themselves effectively—for little to no payment. That means some stuff may get covered better than ever before and that some stuff will hardly get covered at all.

Fewer reporters, fewer beats. Mainly, you'll know if "the paper" got it right—or got it all—if you have some personal knowledge or involvement with a story, or what, in the old days, would have been a story.

In general, as we enter this Digital News Decade, we can hardly find a newspaper, and, increasingly, local broadcast site without some form of blogs, reader interaction, video, and lists. The real question, though, is whether all these facets of the real digital age—the age of inside-out, outside-in news—are front and center, or simply semifashionable add-ons to tired, still too largely repurposed, printed-news-on-pixels sites.

A few sites—WashingtonPost.com, LoHud.com, Chron.com (in Houston), the LasVegasSun.com, Boston.com, to name a smattering—do stand out and are leaders at re-creating the next "local."

That's why, overall, I give newspaper sites the grade of incomplete. For newspaper-owned sites, it's all about trying to find a new essential place in people's lives. If this essentiality is the key to audience, it's as fundamental to advertisers. That's why the other big local revolution is around local sales. (See "Newsonomics 101: Rebooting Really Local Sales," page 62.)

For newspapers and broadcasters, it's about trying to hold on to a business. For the start-ups, like MinnPost, it's all upside.

Two years ago, you could name the local journalism start-ups on a couple of hands. Now you need a map. As daily newspapers have shrunk, a goodly assortment of entrepreneurs, bought-out or laid-off journalists, concerned citizens, and the eccentric have started up new city sites. These aren't blogs, though they may use blogging as a main form of journalism. These are sites that are offering, importantly, new reporting and fresh perspectives city by city. In mid-2009, a fledgling group of them met and announced the Pocantico Declaration. The goal: a new national network of "watchdog sites." (See "Newsonomics 101: New Kennels for the Watchdogs," page 67.)

Visit a big-city newsroom these days, and you may be amazed by the vastness of the room—and the number of empty desks. Visit one of these city site start-ups—if it has emerged from someone's living room—and you'll see a small number of journalists, packed into a smaller space. Or a few editors equipped with the communication tools of the day, talking with their contributing writers, who may well be working from home.

Front Page, Lou Grant, Woodstein, it's not.

What it is, in most cases, is a passionate attempt to do journalism for the sake of journalism, to write stories that aren't being written.

While MinnPost's Joel Kramer is moving into his seventh decade, Scott Lewis is barely out of his third, and he's on the other side of the country. At thirty-three, he is coeditor of Voiceofsandiego.org.

Compare the fortunes of Voice of San Diego to that of the big dog in town, *The San Diego Union-Tribune*. The *Union-Tribune* was long owned, back to 1928, by the Copley family. As San Diego, California's second biggest city, boomed into postindustrial affluence, the *U-T* was sought after by many newspaper chains. It may have been worth close to $1 billion at its apex. Caught short in the local press meltdown and the recession, it sold for about $50 million in March 2009. The buyer: Platinum Equity, a Los Angeles company that has focused on buying up tech-company distressed assets. Its probable purpose in the acquisition: to get at the *U-T*'s real estate. When Platinum Equity bought the *Union-Tribune*, there were no great public pronouncements of a new age for the paper, its city, or its readers. There was in fact, nothing public at all. A private deal done for private ends with the public interest not even acknowledged.

Three miles from the *U-T*'s complex, you'll find the 1350-square-foot offices of Voice of San Diego. Physically, it's not an impressive setting, thirteen desks, all facing forward, share the space.

What you will find in the VOSD office is passion and public avowals for the public interest. VOSD started on a $330,000 shoe-string in 2005, funds provided by retired public-interest-minded venture capitalist Buzz Woolley. Last year, that budget hit the $1 million mark, and the site started growing its profile.

Helpful in that: An Investigative Reporters and Editors award for its public corruption series that "uncovered a rogue system of forgotten government, which was underscored by a clandestine bonus system." IRE is about as mainstream journalism as you can get—serious-minded, rigorous journalists who have been rooting out wrongdoings for decades.

Listen to Scott Lewis, VOSD's CEO, and chief blogger, and you understand the changes in local journalism and their trajectory. "There are so many people so worried right now about what's happening right now and rather than necessarily being part of the solution, some of them are hoping that the newspapers survive and thrive again. People need to realize that might not happen."

So Lewis and his business partner and the site's editor, thirty-one-year-old Andrew Donahue, are doing what they can do. Lewis is the front man, working the foundations and taking on an increasing public profile. Lewis and Donahue both make the point that they are doing journalism differently.

"We don't need someone covering the birth at the zoo [and recall that the Zoo is a big deal in San Diego]," says Donahue. "The three TV stations are already doing that."

Instead, the site picks its spots, and of course it has to, with a full-time editorial staff just breaking into double digits. Two reporters spent a lot of time on the IRE award-winning story. Education reporter Emily Alpert—funded by a foundation grant—tries to connect the dots between education policy, education meetings, and parental concerns as she covers ground once covered by four *U-T* reporters.

It's plainly, in part, about the passion to do good work—and focus on it.

How do you describe that enthusiasm? Jay Weiner is a reporter for MinnPost, who was able to cover Minnesota's endless U.S. Senate campaign last year.

"Now I have to work fifty-two weeks a year to make $35,000 and pay for my own Internet access, phone, notebooks, and pens." The former *Star-Tribune* sportswriter isn't complaining, though. "I am so happy to not be at the newspaper," he says. "We're growing, there is freedom; we're all involved in a product that we really want to make as good as possible. Everybody has a certain amount of optimism that this can be something great."

What it is not yet about is big budgets. Tour city start-ups across the country, and you'll find salaries not a lot higher (and often lower) than Weiner's. You'll find few operations able to support even a half-dozen people.

Up the coast in Seattle, Crosscut, started by David Brewster in 2007, is trying to navigate the currents in what has become a one-newspaper town, with more online competition as the 146-year-old *Seattle Post-Intelligencer* gave up on newsprint to compete with Crosscut and others. Crosscut started as a for-profit, switched to nonprofit status, and supports, barely, a staff of a half dozen staffers.

A little farther east, in Missoula, we see New West, launched by Jonathan Weber in 2005. Weber has an impressive résumé: cofounder and editor in chief of the late, respected *Industry Standard*, an Internet pioneer; editor and a writer at the *Los Angeles Times*. For New West, the local is regional—the Rocky Mountain states, as we'll explore in Law No. 6.

In the middle of the country, we see three city sites funded by the Knight Foundation. Chi-Town Daily News and St. Louis's Beacon have joined MinnPost. Farther south, Mike Orren invented Pegasus News, taking on *The Dallas Morning News* and others, with a dash of brio and database smarts. Up in the Northeast, Vermont's iBrattleboro.com, Maine's VillageSoup, and New Haven's Independent all make their marks. In New Jersey, Barista.net became one of the first independent sites, started by Debbie Galant, a *New York* Times alumna, in 2004.

By the middle of 2009, we saw a new phenomenon—local journalism sites put up by those whose papers had been closed or greatly downsized. Seattle's PostGlobe, the InDenverTimes.com, and NewJerseyNewsroom all have tested that notion. Developed out of pain and passion, these start-ups have had the disadvantages of small financial cushions and uneven business savvy.

Joining these city sites is a group of hyperlocal sites. Seed-funded by American University's J-Lab—itself funded by the increasingly high-profile Knight Foundation—these sites aim to get journalism going in parts of cities. In 2009, J-Lab funded little sites in places as diverse as Grosse Pointe, South Los Angeles, Austin, and Miami's Coconut Grove.

Each of these sites, big city or small town, has personality, befitting its founders and its place. Some take strong political agendas forward with their reporting. Others are better-informed community watering holes. Each feels authentic.

Each also is perilously small. Not only can't they cover everything, there's lots they can't cover, and they are the first to acknowledge it.

For their part, the start-up city sites say, almost in unison, don't expect us to replace what the daily newspaper did. Why? Well, in part they see how the function of the daily newspaper has been picked apart by the Web, which does so many things so much better and so much more immediately—sports scores, business news, movie listings—than newspapers. In part, they are also saying the economics of local publishing makes them focus.

That current local business model and what it can yield is key— and sobering.

Joel Kramer, proud as he is of his fledgling operation, will tell you that MinnPost will never grow into anything approaching the size of his old *Star-Tribune*. "Journalism is no longer a consumer good," says Kramer, emphasizing that the old business model is busted.

Scott Lewis will tell all who will listen that he's not happy that *The San Diego Union-Tribune* is receding in size so quickly. "There's no way anybody can replace the amount of reporting they do," he notes earnestly, even as he critiques how well they do that journalism.

Therein lies the current conundrum, the gap of our times. Who is going to pay the dozens if not hundreds of local reporters to watchdog, to connect the dots, to shine the lights in all parts of communities?

It's not just reporting numbers, either. It's great that Voice of San Diego could publish a great "got-'em" investigative story and get the mayor's immediate and public attention. Oftentimes, though, what journalists uncover can be deeply unpopular, and then the power of a big, local institutional brand's ability to give voice—and cover—is what a community needs. We haven't called the press the Fourth Estate without reason.

Big local media. Love 'em and hate 'em. But live without them?

That's the world we're entering. The established order is fading away. Amid the cacophony are some sweet notes, but they are way too few.

Clearly, a lot is being lost in this chaos and transition. Who will pay for the local reporting being lost? That's the biggest question in front of all of us concerned readers and citizens today.

Let's see how the industry got in these straits as we move on to the twin revolutions—the advertising revolution and the reader revolution—that have forever changed local news.

NEWSONOMICS 101: Start-up Business Models

In the old print news world, you could depend on it: 80 percent of your revenue came from ads and 20 percent from circulation. For most magazines, the circulation contribution was greater. For broadcasters, it was almost all advertising.

Online, it's a different world.

It's very early in the game and, thus far, impossible to describe new *stable* business models.

Yet we can determine beginning patterns. Let's start with a new six-legged stool, replacing the two strong legs that supported old print businesses.

(continued)

The six legs:

- Advertising and sponsorship
- Foundations, national and community
- Angels, investors
- Memberships, largely NPR-like voluntary annual sign-ups
- Events, sponsorship of issues-oriented conferences, and specific fund-raisers
- Syndication

Look at all the models out there today, from the MinnPosts and Voices of San Diegos to the ProPublicas, and you will see these six legs represented. Their proportion varies significantly, as new sites try to find sustainable formulas for survival and growth.

Joel Kramer's MinnPost's approach takes in all of them.

Says Kramer of 2009: "Revenue is about 25 percent advertising and sponsorship, and about 37.5 percent each from (*a*) membership and events; and (*b*) foundations. Projected total is $1.2 million. Expenses are mostly news-related. We do have about $300,000 for advertising, finance, admin, marketing/fund-raising, and other nonnews expenses."

For Voice of San Diego, it's heavier on the foundation side. For New West, it's heavier on the conference side, a business that supports and reinforces big issues and solution-based journalism. For GlobalPost, we see a dedication to making a syndication network work, to making GlobalPost an international news wire of a sort for newspaper companies and others.

We do see patterns, though.

- These are all small-scale operations, neither resembling nor being able to support the big-city newsroom levels of staffing.
- Typically, these operations support a half-dozen to a dozen full-time staffers, at wages below the typical salary of veteran reporter in a unionized newsroom.

(*continued*)

- Full-time staff is oriented to editing and aggregation, with writers receiving smaller stipends. Essentially, the reporting is the hardest to pay for at this point.

One big question in front of these sites: Will an NPR model work?

Typically, about one in six or seven of NPR's listeners will pony up for an annual membership. Sites like Northern California's KQED have parlayed those memberships so that they pay 59 percent of the station's annual operating costs.

MinnPost is among those testing it, having gained almost a thousand members in its first year.

"It's the NPR model brought to the Web," says Kramer, associating that idea in his readers' minds with a media funding model they know and have become accustomed to. MinnPost's home—the Twin Cities—has long been a bastion of public radio support. Minnesota Public Radio gave the world Garrison Keillor and Lake Wobegon and instilled a decades-old habit in the local cognoscenti.

For now, though, membership is just a toehold, part of the mix-and-match business model experimentation all start-up sites are in the midst of.

NEWSONOMICS 101: Rebooting Really Local Sales

We think of newspapers and local broadcasters as strong local ad companies. Of course, they take in billions of dollars a year locally. The truth, though, is that they've left a lot of money on the table.

In a typical *metro* area, newspapers will take in revenue from often no more than 10 to 20 percent of local businesses. Now, that term "local business" covers lots of territory, from service providers like dry cleaners and insurance offices to physicians' offices and painters.

(continued)

Smaller city papers do better, but still focus their sales efforts on the largest advertisers. Local broadcasters tend to focus on large clients as well, with as much as 25 percent of their revenues traditionally coming from auto dealers alone.

Now, though, necessity and technology mean that local media are going after the little guy.

The great print and broadcast ad declines have provided the necessity. New targeting and self-service ad technologies have provided the means.

In all these efforts, we see sales programs and staffs in the process of reinvention.

The goals are twofold:

- Sell more online and specialized print publication ads to current ad customers.
- Sell online products to merchants and service providers who always considered print and broadcast ads too expensive.

The Yahoo Newspaper Consortium figures prominently in these plans for the more than twenty newspaper companies involved, though it has had its share of implementation stumbles. They largely launched their new programs last year, bringing in tens of millions of dollars in new revenues. The two big benefits to local advertisers: (1) the ability to target specific kinds of buyers, like an audience interested in college planning or furniture; (2) the ability to buy advertising on Yahoo.com, in addition to placement on a newspaper's own site.

Broadcasters, too, are moving on local sales differently. They understand that new competition online lets them go after spending that used to flow, without much question, to classified sections in newspapers or to the Yellow Pages. They are experimenting with a wide variety of new ad products.

A new intriguing push here, sure to be more widely tried: offering *local merchants* the kind of social networking tools this book explores in chapter 6, "It's a Pro-Am World."

(*continued*)

We can also expect to see numerous variations on the Google AdWords and Yahoo programs around self-service advertising, with local media "reselling" such services, able to get slices from this growing pie of paid search advertising.

NEWSONOMICS 101: Here Come the Local Broadcasters

Historically, individual local TV stations have been even less well organized and less advanced in their thinking than their newspaper counterparts. They produce a fair amount of news—think local news, sports, weather as their parallel to the A-Metro-Sports-Business-Features metaphor of the daily papers—but they have had a hard time moving into the digital age.

Early on, they sniffed at the importance of the Web and put up fairly basic, promotion-oriented sites. Broadcasters didn't have the classified revenue that newspapers had, so they felt less threatened in the nineties. Now, though, they've seen their own revenues flag, in strong part because of the flagging fortunes of the car industry. Auto advertising has traditionally contributed a quarter of local broadcast station income. Now much of that money—what's left of it, given the Detroit meltdown—is moving to the Web.

In fact, while newspaper companies are now seeing more than 15 percent of their revenues coming from digital sources, local broadcast companies still see less than 10 percent. They are beginning to grow their share of local online audience, but in most cities lag significantly behind newspaper companies.

If they were slow out of the box, they've started to move with alacrity over the last year or so.

Among the changes we see:

• Some, including Hearst-Argyle stations, are making a push to bring in more local user-generated content.

(continued)

- Most are putting up more content. Broadcast content has always been much thinner than newspapers', so though both have made the move to the Web, newspapers' depth means there's more for readers to get at. Now local stations are starting to wise up, licensing more third-party content (lifestyle, entertainment, and business news, among others) and tools (mapping and ticket buying, for instance) to beef up their sites.
- More coordinated sales efforts between on-air and online sales, as more smartly bundled "buys" become more common.
- NBC Local has rounded up its dozen "owned-and-operated" stations, networking and trying to bring a turbocharged national efficiency to local efforts. Other national broadcasters may follow suit.

So why are local broadcasters playing catch-up?

Ion Purspica, executive vice-president of Critical Media and a veteran of World Now, a broadcast aggregator, has a good sense.

"Broadcasters are used to thinking of themselves as *distributors*. Ninety percent of their content is from somewhere else. They have to make a paradigm shift and think of themselves as media companies."

It's tough when you have to make that paradigm shift and others—including the big search companies and the newspaper companies—are three steps ahead of you. So, just as Yahoo has helped organize local newspapers in advertising, hundreds of stations have turned to three big aggregators.

World Now, Broadcast Interactive Media, and Internet Broadcasting all do similar things for local broadcasters, though Internet Broadcasting offers greater content.

They all offer a site-in-a-box, hosting it, adding national news, weather, and the like, and helping broadcasters take their core old-world asset, *footage*, and *encode* it for the Web. Yes, even moving picture people need help moving from the Old World to the new, as they make the big transition from on-air video to online video.

(*continued*)

The broadcast aggregators' game is the same: scale. Get lots of audience together in one place, and the (advertising) money *should* follow.

And that footage? You can figure the average local broadcast station shoots three to five times more video than ever sees air. It used to end up on the cutting room floor. In the infinity of the Internet, it can ride the long tail, described by Chris Anderson in the book of that title. As broadcasters and their aggregator friends figure it out, they'll be offering "extended" interviews and stories, much as National Public Radio is already offering on its Web site.

For broadcasters as well as newspaper publishers, a lot of the difficult change is about culture. It's about moving away from a rush to produce a single day's product to the more around-the-clock newsroom approach the Web demands.

In addition, they've thought of the sites for quite a while as promotional billboards for their stations, rather than new destinations for their customers.

Update the story for the Web? Sure, *after* the 6:00 P.M. newscast airs.

Get on-air people to blog and write? Well, maybe if they raise their hands.

Now, taking the lead from national cablecasters and broadcasters, local broadcasters are trying to create deeper and more inviting Internet sites.

While the Digital Dozen are clearly converging—using the same multimedia tools and aiming at the same audiences—we're not yet sure how much local broadcasters and local newspapers will converge, or in fact merge their efforts, through partnership or acquisition.

Both have strong community relationships and strong local ad sales. In fact, if you look at most of the city start-ups, you see them offering both text and video, and, increasingly, they'll add online video sales. If start-ups begin as more hybrid companies, that's a further signal to Old Media—print and broadcast—that synergy, rather than separation, is the best path forward.

NEWSONOMICS 101: New Kennels for the Watchdogs

We've depended on investigative work for stories that uncover major wrongs and plow new earth. These are stories like the *Los Angeles Times*'s exposure of emergency room incompetence; analytic ones like *The Boston Globe*'s look at stem cell research; or work from the Portland *Oregonian*, the Toledo *Blade*, and the *Lawrence (Mass.) Eagle-Tribune*, all of which have won Pulitzers in recent years.

As with a lot of journalism stats, it's hard to pin down how much "investigative journalism" is now getting done in the country and how much was getting done before the press meltdown. Big metros used to have dedicated investigative units, but other reporters took on "in-depth" assignments. At smaller papers, there usually were fewer dedicated reporters, but often one or a couple got extended time to follow a story.

Time. That's why investigative journalism has been on the chopping block. Hands down, it can be the most expensive. It just takes time to dig out a story. Though it may be a several-parter, that story can represent a reporter's or a team's sole output for weeks. As newsroom staffs retrench, it's the easiest area in which to economize.

A funny thing has happened, though, as the demise of daily newspaper watchdog investigative reporting has become apparent. Investigative reporting is seeing some funding spigots open, and new investigative projects are seeing fresh interest.

"Foundations have made a shift from specific story funding to let's see what we can do long-term, how we can get established," says Robert Rosenthal, executive director of the Berkeley-based Center for Investigative Reporting. His view of the investigative landscape is instructive. After covering Africa and other distant locales for Knight Ridder, he became editor of *The Philadelphia Inquirer* and then managing editor of the *San Francisco Chronicle*.

Foundations, simply, are seeing investigative reporting—watching government, watching business, watching power—as a

(*continued*)

clear public good, and one that should get funding. The coming funding is less about a single topic and more about building a journalistic capacity to do investigative work, as newsrooms used to do.

So Rosenthal's core staff of nine, which has long been foundation-funded, got some rocket fuel last year, with multimillion-dollar, three-year grants from foundations. Those grants jump-started the hiring of eleven journalists to create California Watch, focusing on the state's top issues.

Across the country, the granddaddy of independent investigative groups, the Center for Public Integrity, founded by Chuck Lewis, has been funding investigative projects for twenty years. Its International Consortium of Investigative Journalists brings together more than one hundred reporters in fifty countries to work on longer-term transnational projects.

ProPublica, headed by former *Wall Street Journal* managing editor Paul Steiger, joined the group in 2007. Its staff of twenty-eight has started churning out projects, funded with at least $10 million a year, by billionaires Herbert and Marion Sandler, and foundations.

More such one-step-removed-from-newspaper-and-broadcast companies are emerging. The fledgling Investigative News's Network is aimed at finding synergies and efficiencies among the groups.

Most of these projects, as they should, focus on the journalism. They do the work and then distribute it to the traditional (and nontraditional) Web, broadcast, and print outlets. Maybe foundation funding will be their continuing lifeline. Maybe that funding will just be the start-up capital they need as they master the business skills of distribution and ad sales online and on TV to at least offset some costs.

At this point, though, investigative journalism is one of the few key areas in which old-world declines are being met with contemporary funding in the millions.

Q & A: Wendy Warren

WENDY WARREN *is an award-winning journalist who heads up the innovative Philly.com site. It showcases the work of the city's two daily newspapers,* The Philadelphia Inquirer *and the* Philadelphia Daily News, *and produces original video and online content. During her time at the* Daily News, *she ran its multimedia project to cover the 2007 Philadelphia mayoral race,* The Next Mayor, *a partnership with public broadcaster WHYY, and led other award-winning projects, ranging from exposure of massive corruption in the city's parking ticket office to coverage of the state takeover of city schools.*

Q: How do you now explain to nonjournalists, say family members, what local journalism means?

A: I passionately believe in local journalism online, and it's an easy sell to my family—because most of them live in small local markets that are not served by a television station or a major paper. For example, my parents live in St. Simons Island, Georgia. There are plenty of people who live in and around the island, and they used to be covered by *The Savannah Morning News* and the Georgia edition of the Jacksonville paper, the *Times-Union.* But the woes of Morris Communications are squeezing those papers, and the TV stations in Savannah and Jacksonville rarely took I-95 to the Golden Isles, as the islands are called. The media outlet that does cover the area well is *The Brunswick News*, a small paper in nearby Brunswick, Georgia. It's family-owned; in fact, it's one of the oldest family-owned newspapers in Georgia. And it's not huge in terms of staff or circulation, but they are aggressive, particularly online. My father, a former newspaperman himself, says this small paper is giving him exactly what he needs and wants about his local community.

So what does local journalism mean? It means covering the hell out of your geographic community or communities and finding new ways to bring that news to readers online.

And local journalism is the best place to begin to experiment with a fried-egg model of journalism: Paid reporters covering some beats that are critical to the community (that's the yolk), and unpaid community reporters covering and commenting on other facets of community life (they, of course, are the white of the egg).

Q: What's the best kind of Pro-Am handoff you've seen in your work?

A: I think the award would have to go to political bloggers and sites such as Talking Points Memo and Huffington Post. They are now media institutions in their own right, but let's not forget that they started as classic opinion disseminators—spreading the now-common model of a link and a remark.

From that they've started to cover news and break their own news, which is great.

I do want to make sure, though, that we don't lose the "Pro" part of the "Pro-Am" model—that we don't offer up just an egg white omelet, to overwork a metaphor. This is very important to me for two reasons. One, journalism now creates a living wage for journalists, which is something I support with every interest point on my own mortgage. But I also believe that an unpaid workforce is not stable, independent, or trustworthy enough to sustain independent reporting long-term. There are exceptions, of course, but journalism should not be a hobby. We owe it to the craft and the society it covers to find a way to fund the "yolk" reporting—the stuff that is essential and needs to be covered by journalists who are not beholden to any outside force. I know this sounds obvious, but you wouldn't believe how many students and recent grads are willing to work for me for free, and not just for a little while. That's not sustainable, and in the worst cases can lead to influence by outside parties.

Q: What's the moment when the lightbulb went on on how dramatically this new digital business of journalism would be radically different from legacy publishing?

A: One lightbulb flared when I did a project to cover the 2007 Philadelphia mayor's race online and realized that online voter sites kicked the collective butts of print voter guides. They are interactive. They are updated. They are loaded with links. They build the story of the race from before day one to after election day. And they are available to voters when the voters want the information, not when the newspaper decides to run it. The coverage was not radically different, but the artifact of the coverage—a site, compared to a seemingly endless trickle of inside-B-section stories quickly skimmed and quickly recycled—was far more powerful.

Q: What lesson in digital publishing do you wish you'd learned faster?

A: The same lesson I am trying to learn now: How the heck do we make money on this thing?

I don't wish that we had charged for our content. But I sure wish we'd thought harder about making money online before the bottom fell out of the economy.

That, and how to truly re-create story form and structure for online.

Q and A: Mike Orren

MIKE ORREN *is a Texas trailblazer. In the mid-nineties, he worked in various roles at Dallas–Fort Worth's* D Magazine. *After a brief stint consulting, he served as publisher of* Texas Lawyer *and all of American Lawyer Media's Southwestern products. In 2005, he launched the company that would become Pegasus News, raising money from local angel investors. Pegasus News launched in 2006, and early on distinguished itself on the landscape with smart local coverage. In 2007 the company was sold to Fisher Communications and in January was again sold, this time to a privately held media company based in Dallas.*

Mike, who proudly notes that he has never held a job that wasn't at a swimming pool or a media company, serves as publisher of Pegasus News.

Q: What's been your best strategy at achieving local community legitimacy?

A: First and foremost, be real and accessible. People seem shocked when they post a comment or correction or ask a question and a real human being responds without any corporatespeak. That's the sort of intimacy people expect from a blog, but when it comes from what looks and smells like a professional news site, it's shocking and it makes an impression. It engenders loyalty and gets the community to cut you a lot of slack—when we're criticized for some perceived shortcoming and answer with the reasoning, people tend to be appreciative.

Now that strategy only works when you have an audience to interact with—we've grown that via a lot of content and good SEO (Search Engine Optimization).

Q: You've excelled at using data to propel Pegasus forward? Why and how?

A: We've focused on data for several reasons. One is that it creates the kind of mental and actual linkages in content that provide more context to anything: a story about a politician linking to a profile page with campaign contributors, related stories, and links; a concert event page with audio from the local bands playing; and the like. That means better understanding and more page views as people get deeper into the site and depend on you for more than a story read. It's also, realistically, far less expensive and often has a higher ROI than journalism. Our event page with minute details will get far more page views than a written preview article. Most importantly, though, it allows us to customize content. When everything is in a database, then you can learn things like: this reader likes football but not basketball; listens to country but not opera; and likely lives in neighborhood X. That allows you to provide a better user experience *and* to sell more relevant ads.

Q: How much of local success is about news and how much about information?

A: I really think it's a hybrid. For us, info brings the lion's share of the visits, but the news brings the additional page views and the discussions that make community. I haven't seen any local site scale without some kind of news content; some reason to come back tomorrow rather than next month. I think you really need both.

Q: What lesson in the digital publishing business do you wish you'd learned faster?

A: There are more than I could recount—the top ones include:

1. Even though I still believe it is prudent to do a single market first and then scale, it's too hard to get investor attention if you don't launch multimarket.
2. Ad sales will ramp 70 percent slower than your most dour prediction. But if you can hang on, they will ramp.
3. Perfection is impossible—you have to make tradeoffs on content that doesn't pay for itself, either directly or by creating an overall cachet for a site.
4. You can scale without a traditional media partner, but it's a helluva lot easier to do it with one.

4

The Old News World Is Gone—Get Over It

I don't so much mind that newspapers are dying—it's watching them commit suicide that pisses me off. — **MOLLY IVINS**

But remember, I'm a newspaperman since Monday, and not even that. Give me two weeks to become a genius. — **SAM ZELL, just after buying the Tribune Company in December 2007**

By definition, if you bought something, and it's now worth a great deal less, you made a mistake. And I'm more than willing to say that I made a mistake. I was too optimistic in terms of the newspaper's ability to preserve its position. — **SAM ZELL, sixteen months later**

It was 1998. At Knight Ridder New Media—the just-born Internet outpost of the second-biggest newspaper company in the United States—we pitched an idea for a freestanding health channel to the corporate brass.

Health should be big online soon, we told them, and we needed four staffers to get it off the ground.

"Good idea. I really like it," the company's COO told me. "But I can't approve it."

Why?

"Well, I just don't know how to think about it."

That sounded odd at the time. Over time, I've come to realize how the statement captures so well the news industry's inability to grasp the realities of digital publishing. The lesson: The digital transformation was just too hard for newspaper companies to think about, to weigh and to act on. In falling to restructure their enterprises when they had the time and money to do it, they've helped sow the seeds of their current self-destruction.

Think about that.

And think about the unthinkable: a time without daily newspapers.

As we've seen already, in almost a hundred American cities, the daily no longer publishes daily, having cut whole days just to survive. Hybrid news companies may be moving more quickly online, but in doing so they are shedding much journalistic talent and production. We're clearly into the age of the Amazing Shrinking Newspaper, and we've seen the complete reshuffling of the news deck everywhere.

A world that once seemed so stable has come unhinged.

How did that happen, and so quickly?

What happened to the old world? The Internet, changing reader and advertiser preferences, and just plain bad luck have conspired to wreak havoc with traditional print—both newspapers and magazines—and broadcast media. Despite their sometimes valiant, and sometimes comical, efforts, these legacy media just haven't adapted sufficiently to the new world commanded by Google, Facebook, YouTube, and iPhone.

It wasn't supposed to be this way. Newspapers publishers told Wall Street and themselves a consistent story as the Internet began to affect their businesses in the 1990s. They were convinced that as the personal computer became another way to access "their" news, they'd be the center of the new medium. Conventional wisdom was this: Of course, as people used the Web more, they'd gravitate to newspaper sites, just as they had habitually trundled down their driveways to pick up the paper. First, many publishers downplayed the Web—often the case among incumbents eyeing an upstart—and said it would have minor impact. Then, pushed, they acknowledged that the Internet—which was pulling readers, viewers, and advertisers away from the established media—was having an impact.

They then engaged in fuzzy math, too often seeming like the protagonist in one of *The New Yorker*'s business cartoons. They first pointed to the essentially flat line showing the growth of the traditional business, acknowledging "that the business is softening a bit." They then pointed to the exponential curve of the new business, their own Internet businesses, showing 25 to 35 percent annual growth. The flat line, they said confidently, would be offset by the hockeystick line, and all would workout well.

Sure, news publishers early on urged their executives to study *The Innovator's Dilemma,* Clayton M. Christensen's 1997 book, *When New Technologies Cause Great Firms to Fail.* They noted as an article of faith that they needed to avoid the fate of the railroad owners, who had thought they were in the "train business" when in fact they were in the "shipping" business. As trucks and airplanes came to have competitive advantages over trains for efficient shipping, railroad magnates found they had been outmaneuvered. The parallel, publishers noted, is that newspaper companies should be about news and information—and not printing ink on paper. The truth is that most newspaper companies, though they exerted uneven effort, found themselves unable to successfully transition to digital news business leadership.

The public talk among the publishers made sense: judicious bets, careful transition, reasonable strategies. The message was too easily accepted by Wall Street analysts, including Merrill Lynch's Henry Blodgett, whose drive-by visit to Knight Ridder Digital I find particularly memorable: "Don't worry" was his message.

A very long and agonizing story shortened: We all should have worried. As Americans keen on knowing what is going on in our communities, our nation, and around the globe, we're now on the short end of the stick. Online ad growth for newspaper companies slowed dramatically, and these companies are stuck, dependent on old, dying print for more than 85 percent of their income. There is no way the new business will support anything approaching the level of journalism that the old one did.

Roughly ten years after the emergence of online sites, the first war is over, and newspapers have lost. They're second-tier players in a world in which most of the money goes to the first tier. Sure, a few national newspapers—*The New York Times, The Wall Street Journal, The Washington Post*—fare a bit better than the regional press, as we've seen in our notion of the Digital Dozen. None of those, though, can be considered big winners.

It's a bitter lesson and the hardest Newsonomics Law for many to accept: Law No. 4: The Old News World Is Gone. Get Over It.

It's even tough for me to write the words. Until we accept that notion, though, we can't move on to the tough job of building the new news world. Self-deception kept publishers from moving quickly enough to minimize the damage of great technological change. In the immortal words of my onetime associate, adman Jerry Tilis, who was describing Knight Ridder's follies in Detroit, publishers more broadly "believed their own B.S."

Their failure to acknowledge the mounting realities around them doomed their businesses, bringing them to bankruptcy or its edges, and crippling their ability to compete. The story turned out far differently than they had imagined. The rules and revenues of the new news won't ever be the same as those of the Old Media. We are talking about two different worlds, really two different ecosystems. One is disintegrating quickly, the other is in an early evolutionary state. It's not a minor gap in velocity.

Let's measure the difference in dollars, a highly efficient way to gauge impact. Newspaper used to pull in about 20 percent of all the advertising bought in the United States, topping out at about $50 billion a year. That number has dropped precipitously, to $47 billion in 2005 to less than $30 billion in 2009. That's a gap I pointed to in a report I wrote in mid-2006 entitled *Deadline with Destiny*. It's not that I was prescient. I just followed the numbers and the trends, the same data that news execs had but had put too rosy a glow on.

That report was pooh-poohed by many in the industry—and those who were just getting into it. I could understand how those who answered to shareholders and Wall Street analysts might shy away from the trend lines. What amazed me was that businesspeople were still buying into the industry.

Brian Tierney's group bought Philadelphia Newspapers in 2006 and Chris Harte's Avista group bought the *Star-Tribune* a few months later. Self-proclaimed "grave dancer" Sam Zell took control of the Tribune Company in December 2007. All three tumbled quickly into bankruptcy, with Zell doing it within a year of his acquisition.

They all thought they were buying distressed companies that had been mismanaged. What they neglected to see is that they were buying into a distressed industry. That distress is now so widely acknowledged that few buyers can be found for any large newspaper at any price. Now, newspapers in once-great print markets sit unwanted and for sale. In this Googlely-eyed world of ours, who for the love of ink would want to buy a musty old newspaper?

An industry that had long averaged enviable profit margins of more than 20 percent is struggling to show any profit at all, even with its massive cost cutting. Even *The New York Times* has found itself declaring quarterly losses and having to accept potentially unfriendly "outside shareholders," and *The Washington Post* has rebranded itself as an "education and media" company.

It's not just newspapers that are feeling the pain. Broadcasters, too, have seen big falloffs, as nightly newscast watching has declined significantly, leaving behind an aging audience and falling ad revenues.

The newsmagazines? *Time* and *Newsweek* are repeatedly trying to reinvent themselves as readers and advertisers flee. *U.S. News & World Report* slimmed and slimmed, and then moved to monthly.

Alternative weeklies? They've lost some core business—personal ads, among other advertising—and most have so far poorly translated their print success to the Web. They are more in retention, than growth, mode.

There are dozens of ways we can explain what has happened to the news industry. Let's take one simple—but fair—way to look at it.

Two revolutions have humbled once-mighty Old Media: the Reader Revolution and the Advertising Revolution. They are distinct, but connected, and their combined effect has been astounding to watch.

The Reader Revolution usually gets the most blame.

CONSIDER:

- For many middle-aged journalists, there is an easy explanation: It's those damn kids. Indeed, people under thirty have found the Web their preferred way of taking in the news. Baby boomers still form the core of the newspaper-reading market (average age, fifty-eight, about three years younger(!) than the average viewer of television's evening news); they enjoy the comfort and habit of newsprint, though they're growing accustomed to the Web. The first baby boomer turns sixty-five in 2011.

- Americans consume just about the same amount of news as they did ten years ago, about an hour a day. The huge change: the Internet now accounts for about one-quarter of that time. It's basic addition and subtraction. No one has given us more hours in our day, so the more time we spend online, the less we spend reading newspapers and watching TV news.

- Newspaper and broadcast sites online are far from the leaders they were in the predigital world; now they often place sixth, seventh, or eighth among local readers' go-to online sites. In fact, they face an attention gap, as we see in "Newsonomics 101: Newspapers Face an Attention Gap," page 83.

The reading revolution is not a rejection of newspaper content. Ask someone under thirty what she thinks of newspapers, and you likely won't hear a heated denunciation of them. The newspaper is simply an anachronism. Why would you cut down all those trees, put gas in a truck to deliver the papers, and then have to settle for old news, when you can transport yourself to any news or opinion source on the globe at the click of a mouse or by tapping a few words into that ubiquitous Yahoo or Google search? Why would you go to a newspaper or broadcast site that only had news from one company when you can go to another that offers hundreds? (See "Newsonomics 101: Google and Friends: The New Mass Media," page 95.) It's a revolution of choice and ease.

For those of us who consider ourselves news junkies, it's nirvana. Never in human history have we seen such instant and near-universal access. For the emerging blogosphere, it's heaven as well, providing the ability to comment on the news and potentially reach hundreds of thousands of readers with a keystroke.

Newspapers, not long ago, told us what was important. We could leaf through the A, metro, sports, business, and features sections and feel informed, having the most important stories selected for us. Now, as I do presentations explaining the monumental changes in progress, I like to show the dismemberment of the newspaper, section by section. I start with the first section with lots of national and international news. On the Web, readers seeking these kinds of stories go to Yahoo News, or *The New York Times*, or CNN.com, or their favorite political sites. Recall that Yahoo News, Google News, MSN, and AOL—all distinctly non-Old Media companies—are always among top news Web sites in terms of reader traffic. The Huffington Post has come out of nowhere to reach more than a tenth of *The New York Times*'s online readership. Slate, Salon, the Drudge Report, Red State, Politico, and Talking Points Memo amass dedicated audiences. Americans got used to tuning into YouTube election videos in 2008, and now find they can access vibrant public radio news on their own time as they time-shift and place-shift.

Take the business section. Why settle for a few stories when MarketWatch, or CNNMoney, or MSN Money can give you lots of different stories from hundreds of sources—and all the eye-popping charts you can take in? Or tune into public radio's daily Marketplace on your desktop or iPhone. (We'll explore this in chapter 8, "Itch the Niche.")

Next the sports section. It's still good for the local columnist, if he hasn't taken a buyout . . . or a higher-paying, more secure job at ESPN. ESPN, growing out of a small cable brand, is now ubiquitous on TV, the Web, and the phone. A baseball fan? MLB.com (see "Q and A: Chuck Richard," page 165), owned by baseball itself, is the deepest daily source for news and stats.

Consider the once-popular lifestyle section. Well, its local calendar section might still be useful, but Yelp and CitySearch now have more events and lots of reader suggestions and reviews. Movie reviews? You might love your local critic, but Rotten Tomatoes and Metacritic each shows you what more than a hundred critics thought, and then gives you one "metascore" and links to all the reviews. Restaurants? One reviewer's good (if she hasn't taken a buyout and been replaced by an occasional reviewer whose favorite adjective is "delicious"), but fellow-eater-fueled Zagat offers a better overall take. OpenTable gives you the pick of instant reservations at good places.

Health info? Find a story here and there in the paper, but WebMD has lots of archived health stories and info.

Used to devouring the Sunday travel section? Now TripAdvisor,

Expedia, Orbitz, and thousands of other sites give you trips and tips galore. Maybe household services? Sorry, AngiesList emerged to lead that category.

Adding insult to Old Media injury, almost all that stuff is free. So newspapers—which long got 20 percent of their income from readers through subscriptions and single-copy sales—have been largely unable to charge for news and features on the Web. That means they are not only getting fewer readers in print, but as the readers move online, they've stopped paying. Publishers first came up with—but failed to agree on—an "online pass" subscription plan ten years ago and re-newed those discussions just last year, as new companies like Journal-ism Online brought new experimentation to the marketplace. The fact, though, remains: When the competition isn't charging, it's hard to get consumers to pay. There's enough free, good-enough content out there to satisfy most readers.

On and on, it goes. The general news, mass-market paper has been eaten alive in a free and niched world. For legacy news companies, it has been an odd odyssey of missing many milestones in emerging reader expectations, as readers increasingly feel entitled to have it all.

Old Media thought it was about news, narrowly construed. It is, but it's also about so much more. The Web gives us unparalleled ac-cess to health, entertainment, travel, personal finance, and recre-ational stories, ideas, tips, stats, and opinions. It's about all parts of our lives. Newspapers and broadcasters have dabbled in these, con-sidering them junior to their real missions of hard news reporting. "Features" has often been considered the playpen, not where real journalists want to spend their careers.

Newspapers also figured this new medium would be about text. It is, but it's also about audio and video. Though journalists knew their way around tape recorders and home camcorders, they didn't con-sider those tools of their trade. Now those forms—especially video—are growing fast, producing lots of ad revenue, and publishers are once again behind the curve. Local broadcasters, who of course know a lot about local broadcast video, have been slow to harness its power for the Web.

Old Media also thought it was about one-way conversation. You know: We edit, you read. It isn't. The two-way interactive Web has allowed people to talk, share, and argue with one another. Sure, much of it is blather, but anyone who has ever found a recommended recipe on Epicurious or a recommended blog through Huffington Post or a perfect honeymoon getaway on TripAdvisor values this facet of the Internet.

If the search box today seems indispensable to our daily lives, that utility eluded publishers and broadcasters. Thrust into a "browse world," they missed the absolute importance of search in finding the right needle in the right haystack. Given an opportunity to buy the search company Kanoodle in the early part of the decade—before Google got its search stranglehold—Tribune, Gannett, and Knight Ridder walked away from the table, concerned about over-paying. Even today, search on most news Web sites is usually inferior to just going out to Google and finding the story you're seeking.

The mainstream media also downplayed the value of "aggregation," a feature we'll explore in depth in our next chapter. There is no iTunes for news, and when it comes, it almost certainly won't be the newspapers and broadcasters themselves who bring it to us.

Most ironically, until very recently, they missed currency. That's right: News companies failed to quickly get out the news. Newspapers—grown fat and happy on twenty-four-hour news cycles—were slow to instantly put up news as they reported it, dithering about whether it would hurt the print product or give a "scoop" to competitors. So engineers moved into that opening, often scooping many news sites, which "repurposed" the news they'd printed that morning online. Readers weren't fooled and went where the "news" was.

There's a huge irony here of course. Most of the news content on the Web comes from "mainstream media." It's just being delivered in another form and often on nonnewspaper-owned Web sites and various "newsreaders."

Add it all up, and in failing to understand how consumers wanted to use this glorious new medium, Old Media hemorrhaged readers and viewers. Newspaper circulation plummeted from about 45 per-cent of U.S. households in 1998 to about 35 percent of households ten years later. Go back twenty years, and America produced 62 million copies of newspapers a day. That number was down to about 40 million last year.

NEWSONOMICS 101: Newspapers Face an Attention Gap

News publishers will tell you that the online transition hasn't worked because the online marketplace just doesn't provide enough ad dollars. In fact, they'll tell you that their online sites produce an unfairly low level of ad dollars compared to print.

Let's take a quick look at that notion.

In 2009, newspapers will take in about 15 percent of their total revenues from digital sources.

So 85 percent is still derived from print.

Surprisingly, though, *more than 85 percent* of the readers' time is spent reading print.

Figure that the average newspaper reader spends a good hour a week with her newspaper. About ten minutes a day and maybe twice that on Sunday. So that's more than five hours—or 340 minutes—a month. Those numbers are conservative, given long-time measurement of print reading habits.

Now consider that even the average local newspaper Web site gets maybe eight or twelve minutes *per month* per user, on average. The *San Jose Mercury News*—in the heart of Silicon Valley—for instance, gets about six and the *Chicago Tribune* about nine, while the *Houston Chronicle* can get more than fifteen. Even the NYTimes.com, the leading newspaper-owned site, is lucky to get forty minutes per month.

So for the great majority of papers, *more than 90 percent* of the time readers spend with their companies is spent in print rather than online.

The Web is a great short-read medium, and much of that news reading is happening on sites not owned by newspapers, or local broadcasters. For local media, the paltry time spent online points to an attention gap. While newspapers have been dominant and essential players in print, the numbers say two things.

First, local news Web sites are not essential parts of readers' lives.

Second, maybe newspapers are lucky to get as much online revenue as they do.

The 1950s were really the last great age of enthusiastic newspaper reading. This was the era of a casserole in every oven and a paper on every doorstep. In 1950, American papers were still flourishing, with most cities having more than one. Morning papers did well, and evening papers served lunch-bucket workers. Then, over fifty years, circulation bumped its way down. TV, busy two-income households, and the winnowing of local choice—often to one, "monopoly" newspaper—took its toll. While the newspaper industry was busy reducing choice, computer scientists in labs were figuring out how to give us a sense of infinite choice.

The reader-viewer revolution has taken its toll on newspaper and broadcast companies, but it's small potatoes compared to the other revolution. It's the Advertising Revolution that's really driving the industry into the ground.

Certainly, newspaper advertising had seen numerous challenges pre-Web. Walmart, never a big advertiser, has replaced—and forced consolidation among—many department stores, who used to be big ad spenders. As big-box retailers replaced many stand alone local merchants, ad contracts were lost as well. Broadcasters saw TV advertising splinter as the emergence of cable took money out of their pockets. Old Media was able to adjust to these more gradual marketplace changes, though.

The change caused by digital has been of another magnitude. The newspaper industry is taking in almost $20 billion less in revenue annually compared to its heyday, with most of that lost money in advertising. Sure, some advertising was lost because readers defected to Web reading. For the most part, though, we've seen a quieter digital ad revolution that has pulled billions a year from traditional ad placements in newspapers and magazines and on broadcast TV.

CONSIDER:

- Online ad spending in the United States in 2008 reached more than $23 billion. That's up from $17 billion in 2006. In 2003, that number was just $7.3 billion. The Internet ad industry grew tremendously over the last decade, and at the expense of traditional media.

- While newspaper companies got about 20 percent of the traditional overall ad pie, they get no more than 12 percent of the Internet ad pie. Broadcast's part of the pie—split between national and local—is also significantly less online than through TV. Who gets most Internet ad revenue? The big search-aggregation companies—Google, Yahoo, MSN, AOL.
- The first and hardest-hit segment of advertising: classifieds. They used to produce as much as 40 percent of a newspaper company's revenues and 50 percent of its profits. Now they are reduced by more than half at most traditional newspapers. The Internet—with craigslist, job-matching sites, real estate browsing and searching sites, and auto buying tools—has been too much for plain, old, very noninteractive newsprint. No matter how hard you press on newsprint, it won't show you panorama photos of a house for sale or change the color of the convertible you're eyeing.
- While these trends of ad dollars (and pounds and euros and yen; Japan's newspapers were down as much as 25 percent in ad revenue over the last year) have been gaining speed through the last decade, they got turbocharged by the deep recession. The recession not only took spending on print and broadcast advertising even lower, it accelerated the move to digital.
- Though newspaper companies saw high growth rates for online advertising until the recession, the growth has now turned negative. Even in the recovery, we see little chance that online ad revenues will ever come close to making up for lost print dollars.

Why has all this money moved to online?

The reasons parallel the movement of readers and viewers from print and broadcast to the Web. Overall, the Web just works better for so many advertisers than traditional media. It does more, more easily.

To understand why, let's consider with a very broad brush the world of advertising. Businesses don't want to advertise. They want to sell stuff. Advertising is just a means to an end, and however those means can be tweaked, the better off merchants are. Newspaper and magazine publishers forgot that point. So did broadcaster execs. You can hardly blame them.

For decades—most of the adult lives of these executives—advertisers and traditional media have had a happy marriage. Like all long marriages, it wasn't without its classic arguments: "You're over-charging me," on the one hand; "Your message is the problem," on the other. They'd patch over the squabbling, counting good profits and good sales, and order another martini. Newspapers, in particular, offered a hard-to-refuse proposition: the last true mass market. One buy, able to reach most of a community—and a relatively affluent part of it as well—on any given day.

This used to be the clichéd joke about ad spending among advertisers: "I know half of my money is wasted. I just don't know which half." It has been replaced with one that is chilling to those selling to an undifferentiated mass of eyeballs: "Actually it turns out 80 percent of my marketing budget is being wasted, and now, finally, I know exactly which 80 percent that is."

Recall those declining circulation stats, though, and how they've been declining for decades. The mass market reach has slowly ebbed, now descending toward 30 percent levels. At the same time, merchants' abilities to target their advertising in order to pitch their products and services more finely—with less waste and at less cost—were growing.

Today, it's a changed landscape.

Take a name we all know, Best Buy, the big-box electronics retailer that killed off Circuit City and is nearly ubiquitous across the country. Today, Best Buy looks at its advertising spending almost scientifically. The sweet science it is after: return on investment. Best Buy spent about $350 million in advertising last year, and it doesn't parcel that out to each local store manager. So while Best Buy seems local—hey, you can drive to it—ad spending is driven nationally.

It doesn't plot the spending of a third of a billion dollars by itself. It employs agencies that plot strategy, placement, message, pricing—all in the name of getting the best ROI for Best Buy, the most goods sold at the lowest marketing cost. We think we know ad agencies from such TV shows as *Mad Men*, but what we are seeing in it is the way it used to be done. The new digital agencies crunch and harness data, optimizing buys, targeting audiences, and negotiating discounts with publishers and broadcasters. They may buy advertising direct from individual media companies, but are more likely to deal with networks that spread buys over many cities and sites.

Rather than deal with multiple local publishers, Best Buy and its agencies can let online algorithms create a "multilocal" campaign by simply selecting key geographics from an online drop-down menu. So *local* advertising and *national* advertising once thought of quite separately have blurred.

Not only is the buying relationship more complicated for the media, but the media get a smaller slice of the pie than they used to, having to share more with the digital agencies and the ad networks.

Let's consider another good with which we're all familiar: cars. If you're selling Lexuses, do you really need to spend $20,000 for a full page in a daily newspaper when you know that the percentage of people in the market for a Lexus on any given day can be counted on several hands? If only you could only figure out who was in the market for a Lexus on that day! Internet marketers are answering that long-whispered prayer. Today hundreds of companies, big and small, American and Indian and Russian, are at work to find those would-be Lexus buyers more easily. Again, technology, as we'll explore more deeply in chapter 9, "Apply the 10 Percent Rule," has come into major play.

Just how do you connect the Lexus with the would-be buyer? Well, you can watch the kind of news and information pages a potential buyer reads. You can target someone looking at luxury sedans on CaranDriver.com. You can take profile information, helpfully put into the system by consumers as they register for news sites, sign up for giveaways, and complete social network profiles. Databases, which can be easily bought or rented, will tell you who has bought a Lexus before.

These methods have lots of fancy names. Behavioral targeting—or BT—in which companies place those behind-the-desktop cookies on our computers, tracking exactly what we've done. (Can we turn them off? Sure, but few of us know how to do it, or bother.) Capturing search data: What we put in those rectangles tells marketers reams about our current interests. Contextual targeting, by placing ads near like content, is an older, but still-used method. Data mining is in its infancy, sorting through all that is known about us, what we do and what we read. "Retargeting" companies promise to follow "lost" consumers as they trail off from your site and bring them back. (See "Q & A: Joe Apprendi," page 99.)

In fact, data mining is growing into such a discipline—such a means of selling stuff to us better—that the buying and selling of behavioral buying-related data itself is a new booming business of its own. "Behavioral exchanges," with names like BlueKai and eXelate, are springing up. If you've visited one online shoe store looking for walking shoes, that data is hugely valuable to another online shoe store. That second store could buy the information—about you—and then pitch you with an e-mail or text message.

That's the one-to-one marketing marketers crave, the perfecting of selling in our time. We're far from that perfection, but we have seen profound changes, changes that directly affect anyone trying to operate an ad business to sustain journalism. Looking broadly at the digital ad revolution, we can see three transcendent changes.

The first big change: While newspapers sold space and broadcasters sold time, advertisers now want neither. They want *audience*. They want, in short, the groups of people most likely to buy their products. Gerber wants new moms. Pfizer wants middle-aged males. (Viva Viagra!) During the few weeks before the Super Bowl, Best Buy wants football fans.

So the companies in and around advertising are busy defining and delivering audience.

Consequently, for the newspaper industry, there is no more important ad company than Yahoo. Over the last several years, Yahoo has busily bought and combined ad companies and their technologies. It has poured all of that work into something called APT, an advertising platform. APT targets Lexus buyers, home improvement spenders, and big-screen TV consumers, and much more. APT does that by taking lots of consumer data and then allowing advertisers to pick specific groups they want to reach. It offers more than three hundred specific groups already. (See Newsonomics 101: "Rebooting Really Local Sales," page 62.)

For instance, in the highly lucrative area of car buying, it offers "Automotive Shoppers" overall. Then ad buyers—local dealers, for instance—can pick from SUV (or luxury SUV) or CPO (certified pre-owned) small trucks. Within a big category like "Home Improvement," advertisers can focus in on "kitchen remodel." In that way, those companies that specialize in kitchen redos don't get "waste" exposure to consumers who want to put on an addition or do home landscaping.

Yahoo is using its own sales staff to sell ads. In addition, though, it is partnered with half of the newspaper companies in the United States, forming the Yahoo Newspaper Consortium. So now the large local sales staffs of more than eight hundred newspapers are selling new targeted online ads. The consortium is the biggest growth initiative for those news companies involved. Early results have been promising, as furniture dealers in Houston, car dealers in Sarasota, and department stories in Davenport all report better than average results from their advertising. Those results mean that newspapers can charge more for the online ads—as much as 40 to 50 percent more—and that's new revenue they badly need.

Yahoo, of course, isn't alone. AOL, MSN, and Google all have similar programs in the works, as do smaller companies. That last name on the list has excelled in what has been the fastest-growing part of the online ad marketplace, and that brings us to our second big change.

You know how, when you are searching for something on Google, you see all those little ads on the right (or similar ads at the top of search results on other sites)? You never click on them, you say? Me, neither. But somebody does. In fact, Google gets more than 600 million paid clicks a month—just in the United States (and more of its revenue is now coming from outside the United States than inside).

Each time someone clicks, Google gets paid. All those click payments equal the great part of its almost-$22 billion in annual revenue.

There's an important principle at work here. It's the shift in the risk-reward ratio. Traditionally, mass media have said to advertisers: "We've got a huge audience. We'll give you access to it. Buy space or time, figure out your best pitch. And, oh, good luck to you." All the risk was with the advertiser; the reward—high ad pricing—was with the broadcaster or newspaper.

Google paid search is what's called CPC, cost per click. The advertiser only pays when one of us actually clicks on the ad. Then it's up to the merchant to convert that click to a sale. CPC is only the head end of what is the pay-for-performance revolution. Coming, though still in their infancy, cost per action (when somebody fills out a form or requests information), are cost per call (when a click results in a phone call), and cost per acquisition. Merchants love the idea of cost per acquisition: They pay Google when they actually make a sale. Then most of the risk is with the ad seller and little with the merchant.

We'll see lots of tugs-of-war as media and advertisers argue over risk, reward, and pricing. What's clear: It's a new era in which the technology of targeting, and of measuring response, changes everything.

If audience targeting and reorienting of risk and reward weren't big enough, there's a third big change. It's the dawning realization that the "inventory" of potential advertising placements is near infinite. Not only are media no longer selling limited space and time—the limits imposed by the newsprint or minutes in the day—but now they have an almost infinite "audience" to sell advertisers. Recall the produce once, distribute infinitely notion? There are no physical limits to ad sales, and page views just keep on growing as the Internet continues to grow as a news and information medium.

It's a concept Old Media sellers are just starting to wrap their heads around as they figure out that it may not be so strange that as much as 50 percent of their online ad space goes essentially unsold or sells for pennies on the dollar, "remnant" pricing. As they think through this big change, they're starting to reorient their relationships with ad networks. Those networks have brought them additional revenue, they know, but they fear they've cheapened their ad products overall.

Lastly, the economics of all this have changed as well. Print and broadcast advertising and online advertising are really two separate universes. Publishers and broadcasters will tell you that online ridiculously underprices advertisers. Online media companies will talk about how publishers and broadcasters have been gouging advertisers for decades.

Who's right is beside the point. These are separate pricing systems. Yes, measurable, trackable online media may be more effective for advertisers, and is definitely in fashion. Pricing of online ads may increase, but for now it is relatively much cheaper than print and will be as far into the future as we can see. (See "Newsonomics 101: Here Come the Local Broadcasters," page 64.)

That has been a sobering reality for Old Media. Ann Moore, CEO of Time Inc., has given her own clarifying example of the new law's impact, in a speech given to an industry conference in New York in 2007. She made the point that every *Sports Illustrated* print subscriber is worth $118 a year to the magazine, mainly in advertising. Every SI.com customer, though, is only worth $5 a year, a little more than a 20-to-1 difference. Some put the ratio at 10-1, some at 25-1, but you get the idea. That great disparity exists for all Old Media companies, and in the last couple of years, it has gotten no better.

Quick analysis: There's simply not enough money yet in the online ad ecosystem to support publishing or broadcasting as we know it. So there you go. There's a direct line between the decline of all those department store ads, Sunday circulars, and daily classifieds and the reduction in journalism we're seeing.

I recall seeing the new *Philadelphia Inquirer* newsroom—in its former press space—when it was rebuilt in 1992. You could stand on the balcony overlooking the newsroom and see the majesty of American journalism unfold—hundreds of journalists whose job was to find out what's happening and write it down. It was all those ads that paid those journalists, ads that no longer exist. The *Inquirer* is down to about half its newsroom size.

The digital ad revolution helps us understand the direct line between reduced ads and reduced journalism. Too little, too late, most easily describes the industry's response to these twin revolutions of readers and advertising. Publishers did respond, but their responses paled in light of the feverish entrepreneurialism and sheer joy of disruptive innovation that characterized the winners. Knight Ridder's

Tony Ridder, Tribune's Dennis FitzSimons, and Dow Jones's Bancroft family have been no matches for the Jerry Yangs, the Craig Newmarks, the Jeff Bezos, and, yes, the Sergey Brins and Larry Pages of this world, and the legions they've empowered to build businesses and industries faster than any previously created in American business history. Businesses and whole industries have been built at warp speed by the video game generation.

Maybe we asked too much of these publishing leaders. We asked them—without ever really stating it, without ever really knowing it—both to transition their businesses smoothly and to protect the public trust that newspapers have long represented.

In the face of these massive disruptions, legacy companies are reeling—and cutting costs. Iconic downtown buildings, with presses in the basement and fleets of trucks parked nearby, once anchored every major city. Now publishers are putting those buildings up for sale and dismantling those operations as quickly as they can.

NEWSONOMICS 101: Newspapers C-O-O-L It— C-O-O-L Is Driving Newspaper Strategy

Newspapers may seem like a bit of an old-fogy medium in this digital age. Yet they are trying to act cool.

That's C-O-O-L, as in how newspaper companies and quite a few of their broadcast brethren are discovering ways to substantially reduce costs. It's a good shorthand for the major cost cutting we've seen over the past several years.

Clustering. That's the practice of buying newspaper properties that are contiguous to each other. If you own neighboring newspapers, you can reduce costs by having one printing plant crank out multiple mastheads. In addition, you can centralize advertising sales and circulation functions. MediaNews CEO Dean Singleton is the king of clustering, perfecting the strategy to build the fifth biggest newspaper company in the United States. In Northern

(continued)

92

California, for instance, he has put together thirty titles and wrung out efficiencies. Now MediaNews and other newspaper companies have begun to cluster editing and reporting as well, centralizing functions formerly done at individual properties.

Outsourcing: Many newspaper companies have found new distributors to save labor costs in delivering the papers. Now the *San Francisco Chronicle* is one of the first metros to outsource its daily printing. Outsourcing is one attempt to evade the high cost of employees and often-high legacy union pay rates. Some local TV stations are now outsourcing their archiving of content to Critical Media, a company whose Syndicaster product uses technology to replace labor and reduce headcount.

Offshoring: PasadenaNow.com, an online news site, made its own news in fall 2007 when its editor said it might outsource the coverage of the city council to India. The idea: Have a lower-cost Indian journalist watch closed-circuit cable TV coverage of the meeting, write it up, and publish it. Why pay even beginning U.S. wages, when the site could pay two journalists $12,000 and $7,200 each? Of course, there's a lot more offshoring in place, even by companies as large as Thomson Reuters, one of our Digital Dozen. The company has used lower-cost Canadian editors, based in Toronto, to work on its U.S. and U.K. sites.

A bigger offshored cost savings? Employing Indians in Bangalore and Mumbai to churn out the tens of thousands of ads that appear in daily newspapers and online. Companies like Ad2Pro, Express KCS, and Affinity Express dominate the field; they are signing many major publishers and offering about a 40 percent discount over staff labor rates.

Letting Go: When all else fails, cut out massive numbers of jobs. Of course, it's not just newsrooms that have seen major cuts. Both newspaper and broadcast companies are restyling themselves as smaller companies. There's hardly a job that hasn't been scrutinized closely—or will be.

They are accelerating, belatedly, their own transition from print to digital.

The old signs of success are now millstones:

- Lots of salaried employees. Full-time professionals to write, illustrate, edit, and present, and of course dozens of people to manage them. Banks of ad salespeople taking classifieds and orders for display ads.
- Big iron. Impressive, costly, twenty-foot-high presses redolent of ink and grease that bring awe to little children and old-fart reporters alike.
- Rolls of newsprint without end. All the words had to go somewhere.
- A big expensive-to-maintain building to house all of it.
- A fleet of noisy, gas-guzzling, maintenance-prone trucks. You have to move the journalism and the advertising to the readers.

That world is now disappearing rapidly.

Newspaper publishers, broadcasters, long-time readers, and trusty viewers are all creatures of habit. They expected, as in the cult classic movie *Groundhog Day*, to wake up each morning and find the same media choices arrayed before them: the fat daily newspaper delivered on the driveway, the comforting evening news broadcast at the same hour each night.

Twenty-first-century life, though, has proven to be less predictable. Media executives had cited the First Amendment and FCC licenses, but what they thought they really had was a license to print money. Yes, media in America have been the lifeblood of democracy, but they have also been a great high-margin business. Now that business is over.

One business is dwindling and the other is in aborning. We've looked at how the Digital Dozen is forming and how Local Media is remapping and rebooting. Now, let's begin to look at the tools the winners will use in re-creating the new news business.

NEWSONOMICS 101: Google and Friends: The New Mass Media

You know that ubiquitous empty rectangle—the search box? Google's genius—really, one part of its genius—was its simple pitch to us. One big word: *Google*, which gave us a tickle. And a search box, centered on a clutterless page. The promise: Type something in, and we'll somehow bring back the best results out there on the World Wide Web. Those better-than-the-competitors' results, Google will tell you, are based on PageRank, the Sergey Brin and Larry Page notion of figuring how the relative usefulness of a page is based on how many other Web pages are linking *to* it.

Most of us, though, didn't care about PageRank. The results seemed pretty good, and Google's elegant simplicity rocketed it from cool, new thing to standard utility.

Now, twelve years after the company was founded, Google is an omnipresent part of Americans' lives. About 55 percent of us call up the Google page at least daily, and about a quarter visit more than once a day, according to recent research at Outsell.

Overall, Americans spend about an hour and a half a month on one Google service or another—Web search, news, finance, maps, video, or Gmail.

Put those numbers together—60 percent daily usage and 1.5 hours per month—and you have the new mass medium of our times: Google. Of course, Yahoo, AOL, and MSN can put up similar numbers with their deep and wide Web sites.

Those companies collectively have become the new mass media, surpassing the mass medium of a previous age—the newspaper.

Go back to the 1920s—the peak of America's love affair with the newspaper—and each household took on average 1.33 papers. Lots of newspapers in each city.

Now, with double-digit declines at America's biggest papers, the percentile of household penetration has dropped into the thirties. So, yes, the Internet has taken readers away from print, but they've been moving away for *eighty* years.

(continued)

> Newspapers, which built huge businesses and huge newsrooms, based on being the best mass medium in each city and town, are now becoming a niche buy (see Law No. 8, Itch the Niche), while the search-aggregators brethren have become the mass media of our day. No surprise: the advertising money—more than $20 billion a year—is moving to those mass marketers as well.

Q & A: Jim Kennedy

JIM KENNEDY is one of the keenest news strategists in the industry. As vice president and director of strategic planning for the Associated Press, he has been key in designing a twenty-first-century role for the nineteenth-century news cooperative. Among the projects he has helped launch are AP's Mobile News Network and the evolving Digital News Cooperative.

Q: When you are on a plane and have an engaging seatmate, how do you explain to them what has happened in the newspaper business?

A: There are a lot of ways to tell this story, but the clearest answer is that newspapers lost their connection to the audience. When I started my career at a small-town daily in 1975, we covered everything that moved. I lived in the back of a fireman's house and every time he went out the front door, I went out the back. We were at every meeting, every chicken dinner, every trial, and every game. We even had old ladies stringing together "newsnotes"—a lot like the blogs of today—to cover comings and goings in the rural areas outside of town. A few years later, I moved up to a big-city metro, *The Tampa Tribune*, and we had a staff of more than fifty journalists covering tiny towns outside the city. At the other end of the spectrum, the paper sent me and three other journalists to Central America during the El Salvador civil war to cover the plight of the refugees, who were working their way to the United States and settling in communities in Florida and elsewhere. We were on top of the world and covering it like a blanket.

That all changed in the last decade, thanks to the economy and the digital shift. The economic downturn that followed 9/11 and the so-called dot-com bust began a retrenchment that took a brief vacation middecade but then toppled over into a full-blown collapse in the hard recession that struck in 2008. Also during that time, the audience shifted online in droves, thanks to a constantly improving broadband experience, and brand-new competitors emerged to capture attention that used to be reserved for newspapers and other traditional media packages.

Search engines, portals, aggregators, social networks, and new information sites like Wikipedia and craigslist all combined to expand the news and information universe available to consumers. Newspapers, still trying to replicate their traditional packaged products online and in the mobile space, found themselves competing in a game they didn't really know.

The closest parallel I can draw is to the American automobile industry and how it lost the trail in its response to foreign competition and cultural trends by riding the SUV wave too long. It could be argued that newspapers repeated that same twenty-first-century death march with even bigger blinders on. Game-changing innovation on a Google scale may have been beyond their reach, but craigslist-size innovation was not. They just plain missed it, and now we're trying to mount a comeback from a very deep hole.

Q: AP was founded in 1846. It has been the wire for a long time. Now how do you see it playing, and possibly competing, with companies whose roots are in broadcasting, cablecasting, and Internet start-ups?

A: The AP was actually founded by newspapers to exploit a disruptive technology—the telegraph. Back in those days, the telegraph was a finite resource, and publishers had to cooperate if they wanted to move the news around the country. The digital disruption of today has given us an infinite technological resource—the Internet—but it requires cooperation to exploit it nonetheless. So far, the machines of the Internet—the search engines, software, and devices—have done a less than perfect job in managing the digital information flow. Put a keyword into any search engine in pursuit of the news and what you get will mostly disappoint. It may be a lot more than what you used to get from the telegraph, but it's also mostly random.

Search on floods in North Dakota and you might get a story from Miami.

AP's role in the old days was to aggregate news from everywhere and create a streamlined feed worthy of precious transmission time on the wires. We were created to provide efficiencies and contain costs. From here on, the role of the agency will be to aggregate an even greater body of content and make sure it can be accessed from every possible digital channel. Certainly, with search, we want North Dakota to tell you the story of the floods, not Miami. And our business relationship with newspapers, broadcasters, and other partners will be as much about growing revenue as containing costs.

Q: What's the moment when the lightbulb went on to reveal how dramatically different this new digital business of journalism would be from legacy publishing?

A: I think all of us who started early with news on the Web saw it as "just" a new medium, that is, another place to put our prepackaged products. That was the big head fake we all fell for. The Internet turned out to be a way of life and a totally new business environment, not just another display platform.

It wasn't until 2003 that I began to see that. I suppose it was relatively early, but it took a long time to convince others inside our own organization and around the industry. I prepped our CEO, Tom Curley, for a major speech to the Online News Association in late 2004, in which he basically proclaimed the beginning of a new era. But none of us, AP included, responded urgently enough. It was one of those things people understood intellectually but couldn't translate into decisive action. We needed a revolution, not evolution, and we all naturally preferred evolution.

At AP, we started to get it once we made the decision in 2003 to move to a database model for content management and distribution. That got us out of the "telegraph" mode and cleared the way for us to think differently about the business. Over the course of history, that will be seen as the moment we shifted away from the wire-push model to the database-pull model. In the digital era, it's about enabling access and choice, rather than making all the decisions for your customers.

Q: What lesson in digital media do you wish you'd learned faster?

A: Aside from "It's a way of life, not a medium, stupid," I'd say the lesson we should have learned faster is that it's no longer a monolithic world, save for a couple of monoliths like Google. In the past, AP had to take matters completely into its own hands to innovate—harness the telegraph, design computer systems for the newsroom, launch digital photography ahead of its time, etc. Now, it's more important to take advantage of what has already been developed or is emerging in the digital ecosystem. So, if you want to gain speed to market, don't try to build everything you need. You'll never survive the project management, let alone the capital expense. Partner to fill gaps, buy it, whatever. It's more about integration today than pure development. Leave that to the remaining few monoliths.

Q & A: Joe Apprendi

JOE APPRENDI *is a digital adman, widely acknowledged as one of the sharpest in the business. He runs Collective Media, and likes to talk about the art and science of the evolving ad trade. Joe served on a panel I moderated at the Online News Association conference in 2008, and his explanation of ad metrics was a revelation to the audience.*

Q: What big truths do most publishers miss in thinking about digital content, as compared to print?

A: I think they underestimated the opportunity to have a smart blended revenue strategy, including subscription and advertising. They failed to accurately model the correct mix, what content was for free, what was part of subscription, and what was the right price that best maximized both forms of revenue.

Q: What's the moment you recall when the lightbulb went on of how the economics of this new digital business would be radically different from legacy publishing?

A: When the venerable newspaper icon *The New York Times* was on the verge of bankruptcy and dropped to under a billion-dollar market cap.

Q: How do you explain to publishers the value of niche content as compared to "news"?

A: I don't think you need to explain to them the value of niche content; they get it. They just don't have a cost structure to produce it profitably, online or offline. It's nearly impossible to shed this overhead and right-size your organization to be an online publishing business first. They're making an effort to embrace user-generated content and news, but this is in direct opposition to the branded, premium positioning of the editorial content provided by leading journalists and editors.

Q: What one big change in the ad business should publishers realize is coming soon?

A: The advertising market has changed dramatically in the last year from a "site-specific" buying approach to an "audience-centric" strategy. Advertisers are buying "people" versus simply "pages." Publishers need to leverage their brand, audience, and ad sales channel to sell a branded audience, not simply their Web site(s).

5

The Great Gathering; or, The Fine Art of Using Other People's Content

That is like complaining about a car going faster than a horse. Throughout history new technologies have disrupted old ways. You can't wish away the Internet and the linked economy it has created.—**ARIANNA HUFFINGTON, online publisher**

In journalism, there has always been a tension between getting it first and getting it right.—**ELLEN GOODMAN, columnist**

Larry Schwartz's home office sits not far from Connecticut's Long Island Sound. Maybe that's fitting, since he is now moving on selling both sides of the pond, much like the Digital Dozen we've talked about.

Schwartz, though, doesn't produce any content, other than a company blog, and a few tweets via his well-extended Twitter network.

Yet he is thick in the world of Internet content. He's a news merchant, and his trade has been booming. He understands the Pro-Am era well.

We know the term "Pro-Am" from the world of golf. You know, amateurs like actor Bill Murray and lesser-known duffers pairing off with golf pros, in places like Pebble Beach. In the changing world of journalism, it focuses on two groups as well. Professional journalists, the Pros, are those who have been steadily employed and usually salaried by newspapers, TV news companies, and magazines. The Ams are the amateurs, the hundreds of thousands newly empowered by the interactive nature of the Web. We'll get more deeply into this new dance between them in chapter, 6, "It's a Pro-Am World."

It all started for Schwartz at a Connecticut horse show in 2004. His nine-year-old daughter's horse barn needed a way to get announcements out about its upcoming events. Schwartz figured the Internet was the way to do it, and that a blog was the means. He found it surprisingly simple to set up. "I became a horse blogger," he recalls.

Then, as often happens, he applied that personal lesson to his Newstex business. "I decided we should get a few blogs. I saw blogs linking back to news. It was obvious some stuff was as good as news. I saw an ecosystem starting to form."

So, six years ago, when the pros still laughed at "pajamas-clad" bloggers, Schwartz saw past the sleepwear. As he churned through the nascent blogosphere, he saw that amid much banal chatter lies gold. He got one great blog from a business insider, then working at Bloomberg, who could describe the tricks and treats of the financial trade. Then he found a Harvard professor. Then CNBC's Larry Kudlow. Before long, he had brought collections of blogs into the fold, the Gawker blogs, the Gothamist city sites, travel blogs.

You could find experts in many areas of technology, in biofuels, in video games, and in shopping. They didn't work for any recognized publishers. Maybe they used to work for publishers, and they retired. Or they were professors. Or amateur experts. No longer did professionals, employed by big-brand national and local journalism companies, have a near monopoly on creating the news or commentary on it. No one had previously organized this many high-end amateurs very well. So, Larry Schwartz's new company, Newstex, organized them. He and his team did the work editors do. They evaluated the blogs they ran across in key categories, like politics, technology, finance, energy, and law. Then they perfected a simple, three-page contract, offering these high-end amateurs some promise of a small payment, a percentage of Newstex's share of a license fee, payable through the ease of online payment company Paypal. The kicker was the ability to offer the currency most valued in the blogosphere: exposure and a modicum of promotion.

Schwartz drew on his content licensing experience. He'd served as president of Comtex, which is a longtime aggregator of news content produced by the usual suspects, our Digital Dozen and hundreds of newspapers around the globe. Sure, Newstex licensed those, too, but Schwartz was the first to add the new content.

Now he is Master of the Blog Syndication Universe. Big syndicators—like LexisNexis, Ebsco, and Cengage Gale—get their blogs from Schwartz. He got there first, did the licensing, mastered the content flow, and makes it easy to pick and choose from more than 1,500—and growing—blogs.

Now Newstex has moved on to licensing user-generated video and Twitter feeds, using the same drill: Distinguish the best of the amateur content out there and sign it up. Further, he is now picking up lots of those blogs written by newspaper journalists, a phenomenon we'll explore in depth in chapter 7, "Reporters Become Bloggers."

Schwartz operates on Newsonomics Law No. 5: The Great Gathering; or, The Fine Art of Using Other People's Content (OPC). He saw newsy content that needed to be organized, gathered and made sense of. In this case, he made sense of the high-end blog content market. The market—his customers, who provide news content in turn to libraries, schools, and corporate workplaces—wanted it to be organized. Technorati had been the first to put together a much-used blog search engine, but then Google's blog search trumped it. Both sorted through the blogosphere and made it available to all of us who use the Open Web, but neither harnessed its value well enough at the top end.

That high end consists of libraries, schools, and corporate workplaces that pay a lot of money each year to get "full feeds" of news, well sorted and well organized, to provide to their patrons, their students, and their workforces. It's a world that lives in parallel to the Googles and Yahoos of our time, and there's a good amount of money in and around the business. Newstex, though, doesn't just supply companies that you may not come into direct contact with; it is now feeding blogs to the ever-popular Kindle.

If the resellers of news content needed a pipeline of increasingly interesting blog content, then individual bloggers, who produce the content, had no easy pipe to put it into. Bloggers willingly agree—small checks and a little more notice don't hurt—to Newstex aggregation. By aggregating smartly, Newstex gathered well and gathered first, making it hard for competitors to get into the market. Internet marketers favor efficiency, and those that get something done well and right and on a big scale often can keep competitors at bay.

So Newstex laid the pipe, and that's the classic role of the middleman. As we've seen, the Internet had taken out many middlemen,—think ad agencies, newspaper distributors, and manufacturers of presses. Yet, inevitably, what new technologies take away, they create. New middlemen are needed to grease the wheels of the digital economy.

We all know the industry-leading companies that use the same principles. Amazon is one, bringing together a critical mass of products, reviews, and tools. EBay is another, creating a major merchandise marketplace. Apple's Apps Store brings together tens of thousands of different tools you can get on the Web, and makes them all easily addable to one single device. The shopping mall—the one you drive to—is probably the best example of commercial aggregation so far invented.

What's important in aggregation: having more than the other guy. Just as in the old saying from the greedy eighties about toys, in this news world, he who has the most good content wins.

CONSIDER:

- About 75 percent of the twenty-three-billion-dollar Internet industry goes to four big middlemen: Google, Yahoo, MSN, and AOL. Those four companies dominate. Their expertise: bringing together in one place lots of other people's content, relentlessly trolling Web and news sites. They produce very little, if any, original content. They bring together lots of content with lots of audience and, in the middle, collect the money, mainly in the form of advertising. The money has gone mainly to the aggregators, not to those who have been aggregated.
- YouTube started with the curious notion of making it easy to up-

load and then search for "video." It started in 2002, when most people couldn't quite figure out what video was. They knew what TV was. They knew what a camcorder did. But video? YouTube founders figured out that anything and everything that moved was "video" and that someday there would be a payoff in it. Now, Google-owned YouTube "contains" more than 100 million videos. YouTube is still in its infancy as a business, testing out various ad schemes, but it's key to Google's strategy.

- Facebook took a simple idea that had been around for a while: Create your own page about your own favorite person—you! Millions of people had created blogs, many of them quite personal and quite banal, but they were all in different places, in tech parlance, hosted by diverse companies. First on college campuses, and then more widely, Facebook said: Come create your profile pages here—we'll make it simple—and then we'll connect you up seamlessly with all your buddies. Facebook now has 200 million "friends" signed, friends who spend an average of two hours a month on the site.

- In the little corner of blogs, Newstex figured out how to get to the top of the pile. Pajamas Media, B5 Media, and other smaller aggregators of blogs have all been further aggregated by Newstex. That's a case of aggregate and be aggregated.

- The whole aggregation principle is being reprised for the Pro-Am era. As we'll see in more depth in chapter 6, "It's a Pro-Am World," Pros are organizing amateurs in communities throughout the United States. From Gannett's nationwide plans to New West's modest blogger network, smart aggregation will pay off, as aggregators—the new digital gatekeepers—extract tolls, largely through advertising. Sometimes, they'll share a bit of it with those aggregated, and sometimes they won't even have to.

Gathering greatly is about scale. It's not a difficult business concept. Just think of the old parables about the bigger fish eating the small fish.

Schwartz will tell you, "We're the plumbing. We're the pipes and the sewer." He's being humble. Aggregators first see the need for plumbing. They're essential connectors in building new roads for moving news from one place to another.

Neither bloggers nor readers care about the plumbing. I asked Schwartz to get past the bathroom metaphors. What does he tell someone he's sitting next to on a plane?

"I tell him we take all the blogs and put them on their Kindle."

In this new world of aggregation, news producers are finding their way, slowly. On the one hand, they are learning how to play with and use companies like Google, Yahoo, Facebook, and Newstex. On the other, they are looking to what kind of aggregation they can do, and we'll take a closer look at those efforts in the next chapter.

I remember the first time I had a glimmer of understanding about these new middlemen, the aggregators. It was at Harvard in the winter of 1994. Knight Ridder Newspapers (then the country's second biggest chain) had brought together the company's top publishers and editors for a couple of weeks of midcareer education, in management, business, and global change.

One of the speakers was Jeff Rayport, who then taught at the Harvard Business School and is now a principal at the Boston-based Marketspace strategy company and a *Business Week* columnist. He introduced us to the idea of disintermediation.

Rayport drew a vertical chart on the whiteboard. At the top was a popular music artist, let's say Madonna. Madonna was the talent, the one her audience wanted to hear. "Audience" was at the bottom. In between, Rayport added such terms as "agent," "manufacturer," "distributor," "marketer," and "retailer." Each of these middlemen, of course, stood between the artist and the audience.

Then, Rayport looked at the money. At the bottom, the audience paid $14 for a CD, this being before the era of mass online discounting and iTunes. Madonna would have gotten maybe $3 of that money, a high sum compared to that earned by lesser artists. Of course, we began to focus on the $11 difference.

It went to all those middlemen.

And then Rayport's kicker: What value were all these middleman adding to the audience's experience?

The answer of course was: not $11 worth. The pre-Internet world, though, demanded all of them. Artists needed strong representation to deal with all those middlemen. Someone had to manufacture a physical music conveyance, the CD. The distributors, marketers, and retailers were all part of a long-established and long-accepted supply chain.

What if the audience could hear Madonna more directly, on the Internet, without a CD, and without having to be pitched? Rayport's example foreshadowed much of the emerging Internet economy overall. If audiences could find the music or movies or news they wanted more directly, discovering it on the Web through search engines, friends' e-mails, or the odd tout, such as a blast e-mail, many of the middlemen could prove extraneous.

What has happened since then is that the Internet destroyed a swath of middlemen, particularly in the music and news industries. But it also spawned several industries of new middlemen. Look at it this way. The Internet helped blow apart many traditional relationships. As in nature, after disintegration, reintegration.

Yahoo, Facebook, and YouTube all offer fascinating examples of the new aggregators. Yet you can't find a better example of colonization than the biggest behemoth the Web has produced: Google. Its own market value far surpasses the U.S. newspaper industry in total, and its reach (see "Newsonomics 101: Google and Friends: The New Mass Media," page 95) has made it a center of everyone's Internet experiences.

Take the central premise of Google, well expressed by its CEO Eric Schmidt: "We don't write the content. We're not in the content business."

Google is a search-aggregation company. That term means it focuses powerful search technology on Other People's Content. Its first trick: indexing the World Wide Web better than anyone. The Web, of course, includes newspapers, broadcasters, cablecasters, and wires, among much else. I like to call it prestidigitization, a word describing the algorithmic magic that Google's smarter-than-smart engineers bring to the process of rounding up the world's news and information and making it easier for us to find.

We can also call it the Great Gathering.

Back in 2002—four years after Google's birth—it created Google News. There, Google focuses its technology on more than four thousand news sources from around the world, tidily bringing us all the world's journalistic output as soon as we type a few words into a search box.

It now draws more than 200 million views of Google news pages each month. That's less than Yahoo (at 600 million page views), AOL News (800 million page views), and Microsoft's various news products, but for Google, news is only part of a much larger search strategy.

Recall the one-in-three Americans who visit Google at least twice daily? News is one of the prime ways Google primes its pump daily.

What Google has built is an incredible multipurpose brand, in which the separate pieces (News, Web Search, Finance, Video, Gmail, Images, Maps, and lots more) all connect to each other, building the experience, and somehow, throwing off $21.7 billion in worldwide revenue in 2008.

Clearly there's a value to Google when Google News users come to the site and then click on other Google links. How much? That has been the rub for the news industry.

Until early 2008, Google didn't even sell its paid search ads—those ubiquitous text rectangles that produced 97 percent of that $21.7 billion—on Google News. So it said to news publishers, hey, this is a public service; we're not even selling ads next to your snippets of news. Then, when it started selling ads, it did so slowly, just placing them on certain pages and not on the whole Google News site.

As a kicker, Google said constructively, "And you don't even have to thank us for sending so many customers to your news sites."

Thanks aside, there's a truth here. Because Google's search aggregation smarts were so superior to anything the news industry could come up with, people had migrated to using Google as one of their main ways to find news. By 2009, news sites saw that Google was driving 25–35 percent of their traffic, their single largest driver of customers.

Here we get into what we might call the Aggregated's Dilemma (with a tip of the hat to Clayton Christensen). The aggregated—the entire news industry—couldn't easily withstand a drop of 25–35 percent in traffic to its Web sites if it cut off Google's access to its content. (And Google often said, with a smile, that it would stop showing any individual news company's articles, if asked.)

Was the aggregation, though, really a win-win? Was it fair? Should Google get all of the revenue related to the news it shows the world on Google.com?

Among others, I raised questions about the equity of the Google-newspaper relationship in April of 2009, as Google CEO Eric Schmidt offered this advice to newspaper publishers: "Don't piss off the readers." Meaning: Or anger the search engine they use, Google! I liken the news company–Google relationship to that of industrial suppliers more generally. The suppliers (the newspapers)—or the aggregated in this case—aren't getting their due for the value (the content) they are offering.

In 2009, we saw a lot of public consternation and some back-room negotiating between Google and news companies. At this writing, we're unsure how much better a deal the news media can wrest from Google, and that's a story that will continue to play out.

If the math of the gathering is compelling, the toll of this aggregation on news publishers over time is unmistakable.

The newspaper companies produce the content, getting a relatively small amount of usage on their sites and relatively little revenue, perhaps $3 billion in total digital revenue in 2008. The short, but painful, history of the newspaper and broadcast companies on the Web is that they have been rounded up, rather doing the rounding up.

One of the more interesting aggregators is Yahoo. We've already seen how the Yahoo Newspaper Consortium has come to be a center-piece of newspaper company strategy. It took Yahoo, a fourteen-year-old company, to develop the technology and to herd long-in-the-tooth newspaper companies. Yahoo's work is a form of aggregation as well. The newspapers tried to organize themselves, forming the New Century Network in 1997. It foundered, though, on egos, and the great diaspora began, leaving it for others to organize them.

That points to a fundamental fact of aggregation: Sometimes, it may work out for both sides. While Yahoo is arguably in the cat-bird's seat as the organizer of the Newspaper Consortium—which includes about half of the U.S. daily press—the newspaper compa-nies get great benefit. For the first time, really, they have access to state-of-the advertising technology, and in ad selling, technology is the name of the game. So in 2009 they started using Yahoo's ad technology, and that helped bring them millions of dollars in new high-priced advertising. To boot, their deal with Yahoo also drove more readers to their sites, as Yahoo provided consortium members placement preference on its pages.

So Web aggregation can be a two-way street like Yahoo's or News-tex's, or it can be a more lopsided affair.

The smarter news companies themselves are applying these les-sons, though most newspaper and broadcast companies have been slower than they should have been.

That's ironic. What is a newspaper other than a masterly aggrega-tion? Newspaper editors will go on and on about their great local reporting, but that's only part of the daily package. Think newspa-pers, and you see aggregation: comics, columnists, puzzles, wire sto-ries, movie and TV listings, horoscopes, even classified content that customers have paid newspapers to publish, all in one package. Irony of ironies, they were master aggregators and didn't know it, and therefore couldn't translate the same basic principle—our Law No. 5—to the Web.

Some are moving in the right direction, finally.

The New York Times's Times Extra provides Google-like links to related stories—even from its competitors—right on its home page. The idea: Make NYTimes.com your first, and frequent, home on the Web, because you can get *both Times* stories and the best of the rest. The more visits readers make, the more advertising the *Times* can sell. There are other aggregation sites that use editors to bring together, sum up, and provide a sense of hierarchy to the news.

We often hear the question of what's going to fill the vacuum left by greatly downsized metro daily newspapers. In fact, we know part of the answer. We're seeing a proliferation of smaller sites, some big neighborhood sites, some foundation-funded civic news sites, some analogs of public radio stations, some expanded entries of TV broad-casters. More will join them. As they do, we'll see situations—city by city and across the nation—in which new aggregators will be needed. That's a good business waiting to be born.

Maybe the news industry can borrow a page, or a clip, from Hol-lywood, for there has been a somewhat parallel revolution in film-making. We've seen the emergence of independent filmmakers who use cheaper digital technology and of content producers with no ties to the big studios. The Web also offers these independents more di-rect access to viewers, and offers aggregator distributors new pipe-lines of content.

Somehow, in this still-evolving patchwork distribution system, in which film festivals have served as newer nodes of business engage-ment, films are finding ways into the system and to audiences. The evolving system has allowed such films as Oscar-winner *Slumdog Millionaire*, *Little Miss Sunshine*, *Sin Nombre*, and *Juno* to connect with audiences.

The ingredients in the two industries may be similar: lots of smaller, independent producers, using digital technology, combined with the use of the Web as a launchpad/test ground and the power of viral marketing—and new aggregators to connect them.

So let's move on to the that next story of what local media com-panies are doing around aggregation, rounding up local content produced by citizens, bloggers, and groups in their communities. That's what Jonathan Weber is doing for the Rocky Mountain states. That's what Michelle Nicolosi is doing in Seattle. That's what Scott Clark in doing in Houston. They are all grasping the idea of smartly grabbing Other People's Content—for fun and profit.

Q & A: Patrick Spain

PATRICK SPAIN *is a serial entrepreneur and an engaging raconteur. He has built and sold Hoovers, a company information site, to Dun and Bradstreet, and then sold news research site High Beam to Cengage Learning's Gale. He now runs Newser, a news aggregation site whose editors find the top stories on the Web, write quick summaries, and organize them in a* Hollywood Squares–*like presentation.*

Q: When you are on a plane and have an engaging seatmate, how do you explain the business of aggregation to them?

A: It's like *Lou Grant*. Everyone has a seen a TV show or movie featuring an editorial meeting that shows editors discussing what goes into each edition of the paper. Online aggregation (or, as we prefer to call what Newser does, "curation") is the same, except that instead of deciding what to cover ourselves, we decide what to cover that other people have created. It's editorial decisions without the expense and drama of journalism.

Q: You know good editorial content. What have you learned about the value of higher-end blogs as compared to traditional news stories?

A: Readers are still attracted to traditional brand names. Even though the businesses that run *The New York Times*, CBS News, etc., will likely fail shortly, the brands will live on in some incarnation because they instill trust, like Ovaltine, Zenith, and Prell. Yet some of the most insightful commentary is now coming from so-called bloggers like Henry Blodgett and Andrew Sullivan. The role curators play is to say that this blogger or that blogger can be trusted because we have put them up next to *The New York Times* or CBS.

Q: What's the moment when the lightbulb went on on how dramatically this new digital business of journalism would be radically different from legacy publishing?

A: When you finally recognize the economics of digital journalism, you understand that radical change is necessary. De facto monopolies held by local newspapers and broadcast television news do not and cannot exist online.

Furthermore the always tenuous assumption that every reader of a paper saw every ad, every day, and then passed the paper on to 1.8 individuals has been destroyed by a medium where everything can be counted. So a $15 cost per thousand readers at a newspaper was really more like $150 CPM, whereas online it is still just $15 CPM. This means you need at least ten times more readers to generate the same revenue. And even then, with loss of monopolies and the near infiniteness of inventory, it's hard to get that $15 CPM anymore. So maybe you need thirty times more readers to generate the same revenue. A large digital media business will be measured in the (low) hundreds of millions of dollars, not the billions of dollars that have characterized traditional large media companies.

Q: What lesson in digital media do you wish you'd learned faster?

A: The importance of search-engine optimization and the skills surrounding acquiring audience through search engine and other online marketing. Nothing is more important to success in digital media.

6

It's a Pro-Am World

So forget about blogs and bloggers and blogging and focus on this—the cost and difficulty of publishing absolutely anything, by anyone, into a global medium just got a whole lot lower. And the effects of that increased pool of potential producers is going to be vast.—**CLAY SHIRKY**

Understand, I'm not making a Luddite argument against the Internet and all that it offers. But you do not, in my city, run into bloggers or so-called citizen journalists at City Hall or in the courthouse hallways or at the bars where police officers gather. You don't see them consistently nurturing and then pressing others—pressing sources. You don't see them holding institutions accountable on a daily basis.—**DAVID SIMON, screenwriter and journalist**

When Jonathan Weber moved to Montana, he could literally see the mountains and the river when he was working. His start-up news enterprise, though, outgrew his home office. Now the view out of his office window is less grand, but he's still in the idyllic college town of Missoula, not far from the Bitterroot Mountains. Missoula is the place John Updike dubbed the "Paris of the '90s."

Ten years ago, Weber's view was less expansive, as he worked in the crowded cubicle atmosphere of a hot Internet bubble magazine, the *Industry Standard*. Twenty years ago, he had an office hidden in the bowels of the sprawling *Los Angeles Times* complex in downtown Los Angeles.

Weber's got a new view now, though, and a new perch. He can see the future every day.

He is one of dozens of pioneers, leading new journalism start-ups. In five years, he has taken his New West site and company into profitability, created networks, attracted 150,000 readers a month, won accolades for his impressive journalism, and created a model that many may soon adopt.

New West cranks out an ambitious schedule of twenty stories a day, reporting-intensive stories that "connect the dots" on the issues that define life in the Rocky Mountain States.

Characteristic of our times, Weber has done it on a shoestring, but a shoestring with long ties. The full-time staff, including Weber, who is both CEO and a writer, is about a half dozen. Another five to six part-timers—and dozens of community bloggers and contributors.

He describes his company's four-level pyramid—full-time staff, paid contributors, contributing columnists, and, the largest group, unpaid contributors of posts and stories on subjects far and wide. His pyramid is a journalistic prototype, one that others will study and test.

Weber is one of the new journalism's leading proponents of Pro-Am journalism, a term that's gaining high-profile currency (though a number of different names are also used). Pro-Am is a product of the interactive age. New York University professor Jay Rosen has given us a construct of how it came to be. He early on redefined the notion of "readers" in the age of the Internet: "Those formerly known as the audience." Jay's huge and journalism-transforming point: It's no longer a "we write/you read" landscape. We all know what a Pro is—a professional. Media professionals earn good wages paid by media companies. Am, is for amateur, though as we'll see many "amateurs" are highly knowledgable and highly skilled.

Consider the big, popular forms Pro-Am journalism is taking.

Every day, USAToday.com, the third most popular news site on the Web, gets more than 20,000 comments on its stories. Gannett—America's largest news publisher, with *USA Today* and eighty-one other dailies—has made "community conversation" a centerpiece of its new strategy, which I've explored in chapter 3, "Local: Remap and Reload."

Most local newspaper companies now have community content strategies in place, with some of them taking what is submitted online and "reverse publishing" it to print.

CNN's iReport has seized user video contributions, putting them front and center to help fill its endless news cycles. Fox's uReport, MSNBC's FirstPerson, and ABC's iCaught all employ variations on the theme.

On a local broadcast level, YouNews, produced by Broadcast Interactive Media, is deployed in eighty-two cities. Many stations use three or four of the user-generated stories a week on air. Meanwhile, submissions are increasing more than 10 percent a month, and all of them, from actual news to videos of cute pets and kids, are viewable online.

NPR's new Community Home is its latest attempt to connect its on-air hosts and personalities, and their work, with listeners and their comments and feedback.

Not only is there an amateur revolution under way but also professional journalists are seeing other Pros—like the Pew Research Center—join in with "content creation." If on the Internet, anyone can be a content producer, then many organizations now can go direct to readers with their own publishing. The practice holds great promise, along with a fair amount of peril.

What has produced this revolution?

The convergence of two phenomena has catapulted "user-generated" content to incredible heights. Number one, through the Web it became possible, for the first time in history, for individuals to connect with hundreds to tens of thousands of people they don't know. Then, to propel this new communication potential, hundreds of companies sprang up to facilitate the social interaction. Products like Blogger, WordPress, Typepad, and Ning have made the creation—and sharing—of a blog possible within minutes. Millions have been created.

Number two, the economics of user-generated content are a potential godsend for media companies, big and small. Media can compare the costs of well-paid editors, producers, and reporters to those of "cheap to free content," eagerly offered by some pretty good writers. Now draw a line between the head-count reduction in journalism and the rise of user-generated content. It's not a straight line, of course, lots of zigs, zags, and caveats, but the trend line is unmistakable.

In good business times, the trade-off is an attractive proposition. In the awful business times they've endured, publishers and broadcasters may find user-generated content the lifeline to survival and future prosperity.

Reader comment, of course, is nothing new. Letters to the editor have been a staple newspaper and magazine feature forever. They would roll in to newspapers, and would be carefully catalogued and vetted by the editorial staff. Editors weighed writing, viewpoint, and balance ("hey, one for, one against; we're good") and used their majestic powers to "publish" the winners.

How quickly that era has ended, though publishers still spend a little expensive newsprint on letters to the editor.

Now, there is no scarcity of publishing space, less need for the gatekeeping of comment and instant, unvetted communication. The Internet took what was probably a four-century practice and made it obsolescent.

No longer were editors in control. When I arrived in Saint Paul to work at the *Pioneer Press* in 1986, this story still regularly made the rounds: Former *Saint Paul Dispatch* managing editor Harry Burnham's famous response to a complaining reader, "Madam, if you do not cease this incessant caterwauling, I'll be forced to cancel your subscription." How times have changed. And so quickly.

What is important here: Citizen comment and writing have upended the relationship between the professionals, journalists being paid by Old Media, and the amateurs, the rest of us. So our Law No. 6: It's a Pro-Am World.

Amateur content is expanding rapidly.

Pluck is one of the leading social network platform companies. That means it provides all the technology needed for the media—and increasingly businesses of all sorts—to interact with their audiences.

Talk to Pluck, and they'll tell you that reader interaction usually starts with someone simply reacting to a story. That's commenting—the twenty thousand or so comments USAToday.com gets every day.

Think of that as letters to the editors on Barry Bonds's or Manny Ramirez's vitamins.

Comments are, by their nature, reactive.

After getting involved by commenting, people are moving up the ladder, and readers start filling out a "profile" page, noting their interests. Then, they may participate in forums or discussion groups. That includes everything from political campaign groups to health support groups to sports team chatter.

Then they may "upload" photos or video, the latter of course being the fuel that feeds CNN's iReport and YouNews. While much of the public feels deficient in writing skills, anyone can take a picture or use a camcorder.

Of greatest interest to news companies and their readers are the amateurs who have become contributors. These are people who have great expertise or passion or both—and keep up on topics of interest to their readers. Some have huge direct followings. Some are former journalists—bought out or laid off—looking to keep up their craft. Others disdain the word "journalism." News companies—global to local—are trying to figure out their relationships with these new groups of content creators.

The rules are being made on the fly. How prominently will user content be presented? Will it be used whole or just in excerpts? What kind of links to the user's own blog will be offered? Is there any compensation beyond exposure?

And the ethics? In the Old Media world, editors worked next to their employees and could keep tabs on them, enforcing, for the most part, codes of ethics. In the Wild West of amateurs, editors may never meet contributors or have any idea about their personal or business interests, so how do editors vet? The short answer here is that they vet lightly, and that of course is why there are a lot of ticking time bombs out there. People do blog to advance business or political interests. Sometimes they disclose them; sometimes they don't. Disclosure should be universal, but it's not. CNN's iReport is a model from which the news industry is learning. It launched iReport in 2006, well ahead of the curve. It had seen the power of viewer submissions. Remember that harrowing video from the 2004 Indian Ocean tsunami?

Now, more than 100,000 individuals have registered as "citizen journalists." CNN has received more than 300,000 reports, from all around the world, with more than 10,000 being added each month. Of course, it can pick out the best for online and cable presentation. More than a thousand a month are used on TV.

CNN is also developing new relationships with its corps of citizen journalists. Go to its site, and you can see the "Superstars." Those are the iReporters who are in the top 20 percent each week—based on contributions, popularity, and rankings. It is the Web judging Web reporting, and within the iReports CNN is teaching valuable lessons to the journalism trade overall.

Let's go from global to local. Placeblogger.com provides a good single mapped view into Am place-specific content, catalogued from Tallinn (Estonia) to Tallahassee, an aggregator of "placeblogs." Some local media-owned sites—the new SeattlePI.com, San Francisco's KPIX, and Madison's WISC-TV—are also among those leading here, as they point to "placeblogs." In late 2009, the *Seattle Times*, *Miami Herald*, and *Charlotte Observer* began aggregating "hyperlocal" Web sites in their regions, with the same one-stop strategy in mind.

It is classic colonization—metro-oriented "big" sites rounding up the smaller "community" sites. More sites should take this approach, as they try to regain importance as community conversation centers.

Every big newspaper company is making plans. Gannett is trying to figure out how to best push forward its Information Centers. The Tribune Company is mobilizing communities, as it has turned editors into community organizers. Hearst recently partnered with Am content organizer Helium, which provides the technology to bring in the masses to local sites. Capitol Broadcasting's WRAL in Raleigh is making a big push. (See "Q & A: Angela O'Connor," page 123.)

The experiments are ramping up. The Toronto *Globe and Mail* and Westchester's *Journal News* have used social tools to cover live events like conferences and hearings. They record real-time comments, audio and video postings, and polls, and then add them to their standard journalistic coverage.

Even photos lend themselves to Am strategies. *The Cincinnati Enquirer* put up a photo-sharing site, took in twelve thousand images, and published a coffee-table book, selling it for $39.95.

The Washington Post made a major effort in the exurb of Loudoun, with its LoudounExtra.com site before shutting it down last August. It learned lots of lessons, including how much effort it took to egg local citizens on, keep them involved, and how much the local-local site should be connected to the main WashingtonPost.com site. Getting local communities actively involved is tough, and can be costly.

For the *Post* and other newspaper companies, how best to engage with and "organize" local communities is a work very much in progress. The results can be a bit comical, for instance, as we've seen two different companies—*The New York Times* and start-up Patch—rush to create a state-of-the-art local-local site for Maplewood, New Jersey.

Amateur content isn't just about place, or locale. Two Hearst papers have led the way. The *Houston Chronicle* is among the pioneers, leading the way in hosting smart citizen blogs about topics its readers care about. Of its more than 130 blogs, about half of them are community-generated. Those blogs aren't an island, as they are on many sites. They've been an engine of growth, with more than 5 percent of site traffic attributable to the blogs. In addition, they've helped create new products for new audiences, in traditional feature areas. Pets, gardening, belief, and travel are among the new "channels" Chron.com has created, starting with a few amateur blogs.

In Seattle, the *Post-Intelligencer* already had more than 150 local citizen bloggers before it went online-only, and has made them more prominent since, as we'll see in the next chapter. The range of subject matter in local blogging can be amazing, as Mary Lou Fulton, a veteran of the community publishing movement, points out. (See "Q & A, Mary Lou Fulton," page 125.)

On a national level, newbie Huffington Post has mastered the Pro-Am principle better than its established brethren. It has burst to national prominence, ranking in the Top 15 news sites in the United States. Its success: HuffPost leveraged Arianna Huffington's emergent public persona in a time of great political change. Starting there, it convinced amateurs of all kinds—from Al Gore and Senator Christopher Dodd to investor T. Boone Pickens and actors Jamie Lee Curtis and John Cusack—to contribute their writing. It aggregated them with lots of licensed news stories and it presented a sum greater than the parts—a politically charged modern journal of commentary and news.

Its biggest financial secret: It pays few of its contributors. Its Ams, hundreds of whom did not come prepackaged as celebrities, receive the currency of the time: public recognition of their thinking and writing, which leads to other forms of compensation. Now, in what may a warning to traditional local media, HuffPost has taken its formula to Chicago and New York—and may expand to others.

There's another range of non-household names trying to organize the Ams. Helium, Associated Content, and Demand have all taken the Pro-Am lesson to heart, organizing differing kinds of new marketplaces and exchanges around higher-quality amateur content. Even the Newspaper Guild, the largest U.S. newsroom union, is wondering how it can provide service to journalistic Ams, or former Pros, to help them in this new world.

We can think of this emerging Pro-Am model as a pyramid. It's a pyramid that depends on editors—aha, a new use for editors—to judge, sort, and categorize content. It's not an accident that many of the new local site start-ups we talked about in chapter 3 are editor-heavy and reporter-light in their full-time staff makeup.

So we return to Jonathan Weber's New West pyramid.

He has got that small full-time staff of a half-dozen, then another half-dozen part-time contractors. Since New West covers the sprawling, multistate Rocky Mountain area, he has contractors working as editors in Boise and Bozeman and focusing on important beats. Then he has more than two dozen community bloggers, people like Rebecca West, who does "Borderwest," and Sharon Fisher, who writes "State of Technology." These bloggers/reporters/columnists pick up maybe a few hundred or so dollars a month for contributing their work.

Journalistically, Jonathan Weber finds he can pick and choose in the undercovered, vast reaches of the Rockies. He can find and develop local voices from Kalispell to Colorado Springs and pay them what the site can now afford. He can throw an umbrella up over more than a half-dozen other independent Web sites, in Sun Valley and in Seattle (he has got a broad notion of the Rockies!), and send them readers and sometimes advertising.

Jonathan Weber is building a big tent. That big tent, covering writers and other Web sites, is foundational to Law No. 6.

These Pro-Am stirrings are just the beginning.

We can see in CNN's iReport the start of something big. Some people call it "networked journalism." In this process, the audience, the community, and the citizen journalists all play ongoing roles in gathering news, providing tips and pointers, and adding context. Its outlines are hazy at this point, but getting clearer. Networked journalism requires new journalist skill sets as well, which we'll focus on in chapter 11, "For Journalists' Jobs, It's Back to the Future."

Dan Kennedy writes for the UK-based *Guardian* and teaches at Northeastern University in Boston. He has followed the Pro-Am trend closely and believes that we'll soon see new companies emerging that will better connect social networking technologies to allow readers to find and share content. Among the coming connections: groups forming around content interests; content recommendations based on profile, demographics, and past content visits; ways to "clip and save" content with easy retrieval options, and—intriguing to the point of the digital ad revolution—"pure commercial content authorized or invited by users to match their needs or interests." That's a notion that ad exec Dave Morgan strongly seconds. (See "Q & A: Dave Morgan," page 167.)

In this fast-changing Pro-Am world we see the promise, but we can also see the peril. If anyone can be a publisher, how can a reader or viewer figure out who's paying them to say whatever it is they're saying? It may be easy if the publisher is a big commercial name—Intel, Apple, or Mercedes-Benz—to understand that their self-interest will be paramount.

What about all those bloggers out there without apparent portfolio. Recently I heard of one who was being paid by Walmart—an affiliation not disclosed on her site—to say nice things about the retailer.

It's not surprising, perhaps, given the rapidity of this user-generated revolution, that we haven't figured out some standards, a subject I'll return to in chapter 12, "Mind the Gaps."

This news-oriented, user-generated revolution, of course, resonates with the larger social networking revolution going on well outside media boundaries. Facebook, LinkedIn, MySpace, and Twitter have created more mind-bending social communication change, even spawning that awkward place, the "statusphere." Their users are spending far more time on these sites than on news sites. It's where they hang out, where their profile "selves" live.

So, next up, we're beginning to see more outside-in, inside-out connections between news media and social networking. We'll see more news delivered within Facebook, for instance. We're also seeing more news companies encouraging their reporters to Tweet and local newspaper sites listing those reporters who do.

If Am content is cheap, it's hard work to get at it, especially the good stuff. As Jonathan Weber says, pointing to his long start-up days, "I do get the view of the mountains, but I don't get to take the powder days."

The social tools we're seeing are changing the ability of nonjournalists to contribute to the conversation. Let's now look at how they are changing the way traditional journalists themselves practice their craft.

Q & A: Angela O'Connor

@communitygirl. That fairly well describes the life and work of Angela O'Connor. She's on Twitter at that address and all around the social web. She wrote "18 Rules of Community Engagement: A Guide to Building Relationships and Connecting with Customers Online." She is an online community strategist, multimedia journalist, UGC expert, and managing editor for user-generated content at WRAL.com in Raleigh, North Carolina.

Q: Can you share the 90-9-1 theory of user-generated content?

A: The 90-9-1 principle essentially states that in any given community or social group 90 percent of the users are lurkers, 9 percent are contributors, and only 1 percent participate "very often." In other words, there is a very small percentage of active contributors and a great number of lurkers who read or observe but rarely contribute. Simply put, some people actively participate more than others.

While there is some debate about the exact percentages assigned to the principle, most community professionals agree with the three classifications and have seen the principle in action within their own communities.

It is my belief that anyone charged with managing a community or fostering growth should engage the audience in ways that will convert lurkers into contributors and contributors into active participants. Thoughtful, active engagement is the key to altering this principle in your favor.

Q: What's the biggest mistake publishers make in trying to successfully launch and scale community sites?

A: Many publishers who launch community sites underestimate the incredible amount of time and effort it takes to grow successful communities. They mistakenly believe that providing the tools and the latest bells and whistles will be enough and that by simply building it, they will come. They soon learn that it doesn't work that way, but it is often too late to recover. It is a huge mistake to launch a community effort without a designated community manager charged with building relationships and driving user engagement. A lack of leadership and direction is one of the main reasons why most online communities fail.

Q: What lesson in digital publishing do you wish you'd learned faster?

A: I wish I'd known from the very beginning the importance of microcommunications and reaching out to as many people who touch my product as humanly possible. It is something I now understand deeply, but I believe I lost opportunities early on. I didn't have the all-encompassing view of community across all digital platforms. I now recognize that a digital community can consist of as few as three people and as many as hundreds of thousands, but the numbers come and go, so you can't allow the size of the audience to dictate your level of involvement. I am fully aware of the fact that my audience has an infinite number of choices and that makes me value the time they spend with my product and make it a worthwhile experience.

Q & A: Mary Lou Fulton

MARY LOU FULTON *has been well recognized for her community publishing and audience-building work, last serving as vice president of audience development at* The Bakersfield Californian. *Her background spans both newspapers and technology. She started out in the newsroom, working as a reporter for the AP and later as a reporter and editor for the* Los Angeles Times. *Fulton moved to the online world in 1995 when she joined* The Washington Post's *new media division and later became managing editor of washingtonpost .com. She then held senior roles at AOL and GeoCities.*

Q: You're a leader in community publishing. What has the community taught you?

A: Community publishing teaches you to be humble. There is a tendency toward cynicism and arrogance in traditional newsrooms, an attitude that is dismissive of storytelling unless it originates with the relatively small number of professional journalists who cover local communities. But when you give community members the chance to participate, you quickly see that they have remarkable stories to tell and perspectives that are quite different from what you might expect.

I'm endlessly fascinated by the range of content that community members create. For example, on Bakersfield.com, we have a Christian psychotherapist who is also a local musician who regularly composes songs about the news and posts them on his blog! Now, not all community-generated content is perfect, and I'm not one of those who advocate abandoning traditional journalism in favor of turning everything over to the community. But I do think that we have a lot to learn from the communities we cover, and our publications have become richer through offering community members ways to participate in what we do.

Q: Some newspaper people think blog content is inferior to "stories." What's your experience with reporters blogging, or beat blogging, and how big a future do you think it has?

A: Blog content isn't inherently inferior or superior. It's simply information that is made available via a new publishing channel we call a blog, with the quality of the content being only as good as the effort that the writer puts into it. I do think that beat blogs are here to stay, because reporters are recognizing that they can't count on their business card as the thing that defines their personal reputations as journalists.

The smart ones use blogs strategically to position themselves as experts by providing more in-depth coverage, interacting with people, promoting their work, and just by being themselves in a way that traditional journalism doesn't always allow.

When I worked in the newsroom, I always learned a lot from reading the daily story "budgets" through which reporters pitched their best stories for the next day's newspaper. Why? Because in those "budget lines," reporters had just a few sentences to tell you what they thought and why their story mattered. By the time the story made it into print, it often had the life sucked out of it. The best beat blogs offer that "budget line" style liveliness and directness from the journalist, and that's why I often enjoy reading them more than what emerges from the process of traditional journalism.

Q: How do you now define local?

A: I define local as the common interests shared by people in the same geographic community. Your geographic neighborhood is among those interests, but not the only one. Those interests can include faith, or politics, or pastimes such as outdoor recreation that you have in common with people who live near you.

Q: What lesson in digital media do you wish you'd learned faster?

A: I wish we had placed more emphasis on the revenue side from the start and had developed more local business opportunities based on something other than banner ads that are ignored by 99 percent of consumers. In traditional media, our comfort zone is in delivering advertising messages on behalf of our customers, rather than enabling transactions such as online auctions, local online storefronts, and so forth.

Even today, it would be wise to diversify digital revenue by becoming more involved in transactions and truly delivering customers to our advertisers (versus just delivering an advertising message and then washing our hands of it). With its "pay for performance" model, Google has set the bar for what advertising will be in the future. We need to think more like them, sharing more of the risk with our customers and getting paid based on what we deliver for them.

7

Reporters Become Bloggers

The consumption of blogs is often avid and occasionally obsessive. But more commonly, it is utterly natural, as if turning to them were no stranger than . . . picking one's way through the morning's newspapers. The daily reading of virtually everyone under forty—and a fair few folk over that age—now includes a blog or two, and this reflects as much the quality of today's bloggers as it does a techno-psychological revolution among readers of news and opinion.—**TANKU VARADARAJAN, editor**

The bottom line is that blogging is like sex. You can't fake it. You can't fake passion. You can't fake wanting to engage with the public. If you do, it will ultimately be an unsatisfying experience for both the blogger and their readers.—**KEVIN ANDERSON, blogs editor**

Michelle Nicolosi never thought the day would come. A reporter for *The Orange County Register* and the *Seattle Post-Intelligencer,* she'd wandered into territory most of her newsroom peers were wary of. Online. She'd embraced the Internet early on, serving as editor of the Online Journalism Review, blogging, and just being, well, hipper than her colleagues.

She'd come to the *P-I* in 2004 and within two years was running its online news operation. Like many of the general managers in her position, she'd worked on a shoestring. She led a few dedicated staffers and relied on lots of cajoling of the *P-I*'s newsroom staff, then numbering close to two hundred.

Then the word came, in January last year. Hearst, owner of the *P-I*, was no longer interested in being in the print newspaper business in Seattle. It announced it would sell, or close down, the paper within a couple of months, but might continue an online-only operation.

On March 18, 2009, Michelle Nicolosi found herself the head of one of the country's most-watched news operations. Hearst had flipped the switch, dispatching the 146-year-old print paper and assigning its spinning globe logo to the Web. Since then, she has plowed much new territory.

Given a staff of twenty to make the online-only site work, Nicolosi now runs the site as "executive producer." She notes how many of the traditional lines have blurred. The line between story writing and blog writing is one of them. Sometimes "columns" have comments, just like blogs. The quicker "what" stories are often filed as blog posts, "the Saturday morning crime story," posted quickly by staffers. "Stories" connote more sources, more of why or a how, but there are few "hard and fast" rules at the new *P-I*. Says Nicolosi, "You just kind of know" how to navigate the new landscape.

You don't see a lot of titles among the twenty. "We're all content gatherers," she says.

Readers appear to just take in all the site's offerings as professional content. In addition, they are part of the action, as more than 150 of them contribute their own blogs to the site. Nobody seems to get hung up on what Jonathan Weber calls the "definitional conflict" over blogging.

Nicolosi's *P-I* has offered a fast lesson in reporters-turned-bloggers. As the new site needed to do a lot more with less, these truths of using the blog form quickly have been proven out:

- Reporters could produce more content when they dropped their journalistic shoulders a bit, worried less about convention and structure, and just wrote.
- Readers liked the more informal, more conversational Web style of writing.

- Blogs made interaction easier between journalists and readers, through commenting and various forms of easy feedback. As devotees of Pro-Am journalism have learned, the writer-reader connection made through blogging created whole new communities of interest, and made news Web sites must-visit destinations.

The *P-I* had a head start in this new world, one that proved providential, as it had encouraged staff blogging for several years.

Nicolosi's onetime colleague Jonathan Lansner, too, had been on the job, learning similar lessons. Jon Lansner joined *The Orange County (CA) Register* in 1986. From his early days at *The Pittsburgh Press*, a now-departed afternoon paper, he'd worked a number of beats the way most reporters do. He'd interview sources and write less than a half-dozen stories a week. At the *Register*, he'd become a columnist, tapping out a couple of columns a week and a story or two for the paper. His byline and face were well known in the community, but other than working his sources, he didn't interact much with readers.

Now Lansner is in the vanguard of storywriters turned bloggers. He writes just one column a week expressly for the paper. But he blogs constantly, posting ten to twelve separate items a week, as the news demands. His Lansner on Real Estate blog is a major driver of traffic at OCRegister.com. The impact: His blog now gets more than 250,000 visitors every quarter and registers more than 3.5 million page views a year. In the first three years of the blog, he figures he has gotten 100,000 comments from readers.

Further, the blogging push he helped pioneer now means the *Register* offers five separate real estate blogs, which collectively generate 7 million page views a year. He's now in touch with his audience, and his blog is a daily must-read in Orange Country's substantial real estate community. Lansner, grizzled journalist that he can seem, does not make a big deal about the transition.

"This is short-form journalism. I don't know that what I've been doing is that different. It's back to the future," says Lansner. "It reminds me of being back in Pittsburgh. We put out five editions a day, and we wrote for all of them. . . . Too many people are lost in the romance of the eighties, when we had time to publish [longer] stories," he adds.

Lansner has distinctive memories of *The Pittsburgh Press* in the seventies: "There weren't a lot of master's degrees and not a lot of sobriety. [Reporters] lived for the shocking car wreck. Maybe they knew what they were doing." His words echo those of Jim Kennedy, now AP's vice president of strategic planning, who notes his early experience working on newspapers that once covered everything that moved in a community. (See "Q & A: Jim Kennedy," page 96.)

Embedded in the work of Jon Lansner, Michelle Nicolosi, and hundreds of other daily newspaper journalists is an essential truth, Newsonomics Law No. 7: Reporters Become Bloggers. This evolution is fast picking up steam. Reporters like Lansner take to blogging, seeing that it is a useful extension of what they've been trained to do—report the news. They become bloggers, but remain reporters. It's a trend that will soon transform the news business.

Further, I'll wager that news companies will soon "hire" "bloggers," whether local-local or topic-oriented amateurs and train them in the rudiments of reporting. We'll be coming full circle as the artificial division between blogging and reporting gets straightened out.

CONSIDER:

- There are now more than 2 million blog posts written every year by journalists in U.S. daily newsrooms. That's a conservative number I've computed by taking the 1,500 or so daily papers and estimating that each of those papers has fifteen reporters or editors blogging. Then, let's say each writes just two posts a week. And we'll give them a couple of weeks off for vacation. The number of blogging journalists and their output is probably low. Still, we get 2.25 million blog posts a year.
- Many newspapers—the *San Jose Mercury News* was one of the first—are starting to pick up selected blog posts and put them in the daily paper, "cut and pasted." That's another form of "reverse publishing."
- Jon Lansner's experience is typical; journalists who take to blogging as a form usually produce more content for their employers.

That should mean more revenue for their employers, though it hasn't yet.

- As story writing in newspapers has decreased—I estimate that production of stories is down at least 20 percent in the last five years—"post" production is up. Where, when, and how will the lines cross?

- While news companies are taking to blogs, most have been slow to incorporate them in the mainstream of their work, their products—and their ad sales.

- *Newsweek*, in a struggle to redefine its essence, has strongly embraced "staff" blogging as it tries to become the U.S.'s *Economist*.

- If the traditional press doesn't use the blogging tools quickly enough, many others are eager to, and they are breaking news, left and right. Blog-first scribes from Huffington Post, Slate, Salon, Talking Points Memo, Hot Air, PoliPundit, and Politico, among many others, understand the value of the post intuitively. These sites are showing the way in combining pointed writing and personality. BlogNetNews, put together by former daily editorial writer Dave Mastio, catalogues hundreds of newsy bloggers across the United States.

Still confusion reigns in many newsrooms.

We all know what news is, right? Blogs are something else again. They can report from the grimy streets of Basra or comment on Aunt Lilly's kimono collection. While anyone can write a blog, a journalist can write a story or a blog. So what's a story? We think of stories as something that traditional media do, in a newspaper or a magazine or on air. A blog, well that's something you do for the Internet. The distinction, though, is crazy making.

If Jon Lansner uses different software to write a blog post for OCRegister.com than he does to write a column for the print *Register*—and yes, the software is usually different—is that an important distinction? Of course not. Is he any less a journalist? Of course not.

Among those agreeing and attempting to end the artificial distinction between newsroom story writing and newsroom blogging is Jonathan Landman of *The New York Times*. Blogging has become a more important tool at the *Times*. NYtimes.com now hosts more than seventy blogs. Twenty of those blogs present opinion or commentary. More than fifty focus on news and information. Reporter Tara Parker-Pope writes on health; David Carr writes on media; and David Pogue on personal tech.

For the *Times*, Landman says, blogging is more like another tool than a distinct form of journalism. "I don't think of it as separate. People make too much of what's a real blog. Is it snarky, personal?" More important is what the blog format can offer journalists—immediacy, informality, interactivity.

Blogs are in their infancy at the *Times*, but they already represent about 5 percent of the *Times* site's traffic. Typically, at the *Times*, about ten blogs draw more than one million page views in a month, half of those pulling in 2 million, and a few totaling more than 3 million. Which blogs make it into the top ten, though, can vary with the news.

One of the *Times*'s nearby competitors has embraced blogging even more fully. It is helping Henry Freeman's LoHud.com (for Lower Hudson Valley) distinguish itself from its journalistic peers. Freeman is the editor of the Gannett-owned *Journal News* in Westchester, a large suburban county north of New York City. The *Journal News* competes with lots of media, while maintaining a daily circulation of about 95,000. One of its key competitive strategies: staff blogging. It sports fifty local blogs.

Some of them bust out. Peter Abraham was the first reporter in the New York City area to start a Yankees blog. His blog—The LoHud Yankees Blog—now does gangbusters traffic, especially if you line up his paper's relatively small circulation against the bigger dailies a little to the south.

I talked to Henry Freeman just as baseball season was getting under way last year. His enthusiasm spilled into a string of e-mails. Among them: "Our Yankees blog has had 243,680 page views and 5,552 comments on blog postings over the last forty-eight hours. Those are incredible numbers, even for the Yankees.

"The reason is the Yankees are playing the Red Sox and Peter Abraham, our Yankees beat writer, reached out to the writer of the Red Sox blog on WEEI.com in Boston. The two bloggers have been cross-promoting the posts on each of the blogs. It has gotten the fan bases of each team interacting and the results have increased traffic for both sites. We may do a podcast with them for the next series."

Now here is an editor who gets it, and is promoting it. Freeman says that about 20 percent of LoHud's site traffic is driven by blogs, the highest number I've heard.

Freeman says that bloggers get some basic training and some guidelines. Post at least daily, they are told, and most exceed that number. Peter Abraham may write fifteen to twenty a day.

How does Freeman explain the post-story difference? "Report for the Web, write for the paper," he says, acknowledging that the line is often fairly blurred, but that the staff, as in Seattle, is learning what works. As Gannett works out its own transformation, it is looking to Westchester as a model.

Blogging is certainly a useful individual tool. Journalists are also testing the ins and outs of beat blogging. Beat blogging draws together several reporters to work on a single subject and connects them with the audience interested in and often deeply knowledgable about it.

The *Times* has applied beat blogging to business deal making (DealBook) and politics (The Caucus). The latter peaked at 18 million page views in October 2008 just before the presidential election. Deal Book, of course, is in head-to-head competition with *The Wall Street Journal*'s "Heard on the Street," the longtime print feature that saw a significant reporting and Web expansion last year. "Heard on the Street," on the WSJ.com Web site, of course, is now beat blogging as well.

Gannett's Kate Marymont is another proponent of beat blogging. She has seen it work as Gannett papers used it around community child-safety issues. "It's a tool for connecting all the different players—county, state, federal officials. They were tripping all over each other." On the Web site, "They were sharing, and the public was watching." Now she says beat blogging is morphing as Gannett's newspapers experiment with using Twitter and Facebook to connect up journalists and the community around big stories and issues.

In fact, across the country, we see reporters and writers now taking to Twitter—as a research and interviewing tool—much more quickly than they took to blogging. It's the bloggers, first, who have understood that Twitter really is "microblogging" (140 characters) and that once you've started down the blogging path, you may as well pick up the latest tricks of the trade.

The Washington Post has taken a longtime reader favorite—obituaries—and turned it into a beat blog, Post Mortem. It's done by its team of four writers, and it's lively.

If blogging is gradually being accepted as a tool, we can see how most media companies' slow uptake is hurting them. First off, they are leaving money on the table, as we can see when we look at the math of blogging.

A little Newsonomics math: How much more valuable are bloggers than story-writing journalists? Well, it depends, of course, on how much content they produce, of what immediacy, quality, and reader interest.

Let's take Jon Lansner's work in Orange County as an example. Before he started blogging, Lansner wrote an average of three columns or stories a week. Each of these would typically fit on one page. When a reader clicks to that page, that's a page view.

Just as with David Pogue's example in chapter 2, let's say that there are three ads on that page. Let's say each ad in real-estate-oriented Orange County averages $5 CPM (cost per thousand page views). Given the subprime meltdown vagaries of real estate, that number should well be higher over time, but let's shoot low.

So *The Orange County Register* should be able to sell three ads with a $5 CPM on Lansner's pages. Let's say each story or post gets 10,000 page views a month. At $15 (three ads at $5 CPM), that's $150 in online ad revenue per story. So if he writes three stories a week, that's thirteen stories a month. Do the math and you can see how the *Register* could take in $1,950 in revenue a month.

Now, let's remember that, in blogging, Jon Lansner is creating two to three times more content than he did as a story writer or column writer. So let's use a multiplier of roughly 2.5. Let's say he writes about thirty-two separate posts a month (that's about what he averages). Let's say that each post gets the same number of page views and that advertising sells for the same price; after all, it's the same journalist writing about the same subject. Multiply it out and the *Register* could take in $4,875 a month, as compared to $1,950. That's a big difference. Presumably, the *Register* isn't paying its bloggers more than its story writers or columnists, but maybe it should.

Of course, there are unknowns here.

- Will posts get the same, fewer, or more page views? Lansner's increasing popularity, tied to the interactive nature of his work—remember, he got 30,000 comments a year—should mean he gets more page views. In this exercise, though, we've held the number constant.
- Will more page views result in more advertising? Probably, but not necessarily proportionately.
- Should the *Register* be able to profit on the blog switch? In a normal economy, we'd think yes.

The math, though, is clear: Multiply out those numbers across companies and across the country, and we're talking about hundreds of millions of dollars in added revenue.

Each blogger's work quality, timeliness, popularity, and subject matter will determine how much a differential publishers gain from turning story writers into bloggers. Here Law No. 8, Itch the Niche, is hugely important, as is the old standby, quality.

So by this measure, at least, good bloggers are more valuable than good story writers.

One of the reasons publishers have been slow to move on these simple economics is how they sell advertising. Their ad sellers often don't understand blogs, and undersell them. No surprise here; that's part of the blog-story confusion.

Look at the economics, though, as we just did, and you'd think publishers and broadcasters—who are as slow to learn this lesson as their print colleagues—would smarten up more quickly and educate their selling staffs and perhaps reluctant ad buyers. Advertising targeting here clearly trails reader adoption.

Lastly, of course, there are "craft" issues with staff blogging. We often hear silly industry arguments that blogs are inferior because "they are not edited." Well, then, go ahead and edit them, I say. There's no rule saying that blogs can't be edited by one or by a dozen people. Sure, they usually get lighter editing because they're less formal, and profit from immediacy—and they can quickly be corrected when some wise reader points out a miscue. Whether they are edited, though, that's an internal decision.

Blog writing has unearthed some truths in journalism's underbelly. Sure, readers like the immediacy, the interactivity, and the informality. They also like and appreciate, though, the dropping of pretension. No, not every story has two equal sides, as the now-musty traditions of monopoly daily journalism tried to impose. Some have more than two sides; some don't have sides at all. The journalist's job is to report what she hears, sees, weighs, and checks. If blogging helps push journalists to do that job better—and drop the pretense that sticking a virtual microphone in front of two warring sides constitutes reporting—then it will have done us a service.

We're into a time of redefinitions. As an analyst, I talk frequently to the press that covers the news industry. Increasingly, those reporters from such Digital Dozen companies as *The New York Times* and Reuters are using blogging themselves, as part of their official duties. So I'm a journalist-turned-analyst who talks to journalists who blog.

Confusing? Sounds from the outside like it might be, but, surprisingly, it's not.

Journalism is based on trust. Trust between readers and journalists, though that often gets tested. Trust between journalists and sources. The common denominator—what we're taught in journalism school and what readers will tell you they want—is fairness. You don't break a trust, so you're careful.

To the extent that principle carries over to the Web, we're in good shape, though it certainly is ungainly out there, with all kinds of writers, some journalists, some advocates, some in the pocket of various industries, causes, and initiatives.

It can be confusing, but a look at the flip side helps here. Just as anyone can say or write anything on the Web, anybody can be critiqued—and instantly. Break a trust, misrepresent a subject—and many people will be all over you.

The new environment tells us we're far beyond the Woodward and Bernstein era of institutional got-'em investigative journalism, but it's an evolving balance we're seeing. How effective will it be, compared to old methods of vetting? At this point, in truth, we have too little idea and too little experience.

If journalism is the first rough draft of history, as Phil Graham, the former publisher of *The Washington Post*, reportedly said, then is blogging the first draft of the first draft?

So user-generated content and blogging are two of the factors changing how we read and what we read. Let's move on to look at what we call news itself, and note the passing of the time of "general news."

8

Itch the Niche

We journalists make it a point to know very little about an extremely wide variety of topics; this is how we stay objective.—**DAVE BARRY, humorist**

The future has arrived. It's just not evenly distributed.—**WILLIAM GIBSON, novelist**

J. J. Yore is no household name, though from his offices in the Bunker Hill neighborhood of downtown L.A., not far from the Staples Center, he runs what may be the most-listened-to business news broadcast operation in the United States. If you listen to public radio, odds are you've heard one of his programs; they're hard to miss. As the executive producer of Marketplace, he has nurtured one of the fastest-growing business news franchises in the country. Business news? On public radio?

Yes, the thought would have sounded silly a couple of decades ago. Now, though, Marketplace is becoming ubiquitous. From its inception in 1996, Marketplace rode the economy waves up and down, into the bubble and its bursting, and then again through the boom years and the trough of deep recession.

The half-hour, five-day-a-week, post-stock-market-close Marketplace is the flagship, distributed on more than three hundred public radio stations across the country. The get-ready-for-the-business-day

Marketplace Morning launched in 2007. Marketplace Money, a weekly personal finance show, is part of the stable.

Marketplace isn't just radio; it's audio, and its podcasts are among the Top 10 in the iTunes App Store. Its online site features explainers and gizmos—The Decoder, Whiteboard, and special reports.

Marketplace serves a radio audience that didn't much exist a short time ago. It was the brainchild of Jim Russell, who saw a market need. It serves up intelligent, sprightly coverage of the news day through the prism of money and in such a way that mere non-MBA'ed mortals can understand it.

So we come to Law No. 8, Itch the Niche. Business news is a niche. J. J. Yore and Jim Russell itched it, and created something new. The digital news business, it turns out, is all about niches.

It's not hard to understand why. When was the last time you heard somebody say, "I want more news!" We've seen throughout this book that we live in a news bubble in which we can't help but know the big news of the day. What we want more of is what *we're* interested in, but which the next guy may find boring.

When we say we want to know more about seasonal Hawaii getaways, we've entered the travel niche. When we need information on what to do about a bad cough, we've entered the health niche. When we want to know how our team is doing, we've entered sports.

As we've seen in chapter 4, newspapers and broadcasters in the past gave us a little about a lot of subjects. In fact, anyone who has been in one of those newsrooms knows where everyone starts and everyone takes pride in being able to do: general assignment. The conceit: Any reporter can write about anything, and he'll bring back a decent story. Sure, there were always metro reporters and sports reporters and, later, business reporters, but any newspaper reporter worth his salt knew that being tossed into any story—unprepared—and bringing it back alive was the mark of a newspaperman.

That worked for a long time. In its belief, we can see the flourishing—and now the decline—of the mass-pleasing daily newspaper. The old idea: Something for everyone, a good compilation of the news of the day before. The Internet changed all that. The Internet has made specialized reading easier, and, consequently, it is making specialized reporting and writing more valuable. The Web is tailor-made to easily gather a lot of information about any subject no matter how narrow.

For media companies, it's a happy coincidence that niche audience interests match up well with targeted advertising—the whole goal of that digital ad revolution described in chapter 4—and that's why itching the niche is a primary focus of all modern media companies.

Consider:

Niches produce significantly higher advertising rates and sales than does "news." In fact, if you drew a pyramid, you'd find business news at the top, often outdrawing "news" ad pricing four or five times to one. Below business is technology, health, and travel. Toward the bottom: "news."

The Wall Street Journal and *The New York Times* are two of the latest entrants in the niche "luxury" market. In the midst of recession, the *Journal* launched the occasional glossy magazine *WSJ* to compete against the *Times*'s stable of *T* publications, focusing on fashion, jewelry, and high style.

Even local newspaper companies are focusing on niche, as both MediaNews and Lee Enterprises, each with more than fifty dailies, have set goals to expand niche print publications as they wind down mass print—the daily newspaper. Advertisers love "buying" niches like weddings, home improvement, financial planning, and college selection. The key: Find a niche in which lots of money changes hands, and you've got a winner.

The niche movement is universal. Who has lost audience for years? The Big Three television networks. Who has gained? The limitless world of cable. Call it splintered—food, fashion, travel, adventure, home design, golf, tennis—or call it niched. Magazines? The general news magazines have fared the worst, as they lose readership and advertising, while niches have done better. While mass general daily newspaper companies are hemorrhaging, the ethnic press is doing well. Every conceivable niche is being reimagined. Even science news has experienced a great upheaval, as we see in Nancy Shute's Q & A, page 153.

News companies, of course, aren't alone in pursuing lucrative niches. Just take the area of major league sports, for instance, and you can see how MLB, the NHL, and the NFL are all usurping roles formerly played by local and national media.

Business news niching offers us a to-the-point primer.

Business. If Depression-era bank robber Willie Sutton (*Q:* "Willie, why do you rob banks?" *A:* "That's where the money is.") were alive today, he'd avoid the wounded financial institutions and head right for online business journalism.

The Web and business news are a match made in heaven. Business is about immediacy, moving much faster than many other sectors (government, local events, even entertainment and sports) with coverage measurable in seconds, minutes, hours, and days. Business is about numbers, and we now have instant access to interactive, constantly updating databases.

For the daily press, that has created a headache. Business news sections had been an audience builder and moneymaker since the 1980s. Both weekly business sections (often "Business Monday" tabs) and daily sections whetted the growing middle-class investor appetite and made business more interesting.

The Internet first changed that reader connection as digital stock listings made pages of tables obsolescent, and publishers replaced them with real-time digital portfolios. For the first time, we could see much of our net worth at a glance; it was a fun sport while the stock market boom lasted. Then it dawned on everyone: Much business news is national and global, and that has allowed the Digital Dozen (Law No. 2) to provide news and data *directly* to local customers.

So the audience and the dollars have moved quickly online, and that has greatly reduced local daily business coverage. Dozens of metro-sized dailies, from the *St. Petersburg Times* to *The Orange County Register* to *The Denver Post* have dropped stand-alone business sections within the last year. Many other dailies have substantially cut back business news space and reporting staff, as formerly robust sections thinned to a sad four pages.

But the business and finance ad opportunity on the Web is large. The U.S. Interactive Advertising Bureau shows business and finance as the second-largest category (behind only retail advertising generally) for revenue, representing about 15 percent of online advertising spending, or more than $3 billion. Further, financial advertisers are now spending more than one in five of their dollars online. Not all of that spending goes to business news sites, but about a billion dollars a year does.

That's why we've seen increased head-butting between competitors, even through the recession. Rupert Murdoch kicked off the new round of competition when his News Corporation paid $5.6 billion, a 60 percent "premium," to acquire Dow Jones in 2007. He'd bagged the top business newspaper in the world, *The Wall Street Journal*. His declared intention: to make the *Journal* and its sister business publications (*Barron's*, MarketWatch) into a truly global and cross-platform franchise (newsprint, cable, satellite, Web, mobile). In September 2009, News Corp. announced "NewsCore," an initiative designed to bring together all that content for use throughout the company.

The recession slowed down Murdoch's Dow Jones investment plans, but still the *Journal* has aimed bigger guns at the company Murdoch lives to hate: *The New York Times*. For years, the *Times* has been the serious, national American paper; the *Journal* has been the serious national American *business* paper. Murdoch immediately blurred those boundaries, focusing the *Journal*'s front page more on the biggest news, business or not. He staffed up national and international reporting in general, even devoting more space to it, and added a daily sports page.

For its part, the *Times*, even as it reeled due to 25 percent advertising revenue declines, beefed up its business and technology coverage.

Every day, you can see the warriors go at it online, as the *Journal*'s expanded, iconic "Heard on the Street" does battle with the *Times*'s expanded "DealBook."

When Murdoch bought Dow Jones, he said one of the reasons he found it compelling was that it focused on business content, and that was news "you could charge for." That's the value of a niche in which information can make or break a pocketbook or a balance sheet.

While the *Journal* and the *Times* necessarily focus on each other, other business news competitors have been redeploying their armies, too. Many are headquartered just blocks away in Manhattan.

There's Bloomberg. Long before Michael Bloomberg became New York's mayor, "the Bloomberg" terminal sat in financial companies, Fortune 500 firms overall, and newsrooms everywhere. The Bloomberg machine displayed the fastest, most accurate business data and quick takes on it, and it has managed to survive the open Internet. Still, 90 percent of Bloomberg's revenue derives from these proprietary terminals, though it has invested tens of millions of dollars and hundreds of staffers to extend the Bloomberg brand to TV, radio, mobile, and the Web. It just bought long-established *Business Week*.

Bloomberg may have its TV niche, but it's CNBC that has staked out the business news and commentary lead there. It has been joined by another Murdoch-owned business operation, the small, but growing Fox Business Network.

You can't forget two other Digital Dozen stalwarts, Thomson Reuters and AP, both of them "wires." Only 10 percent of Thomson Reuters revenues are driven by its news wire; a large part devolves from financial reporting and data. AP, its wire competitor, offers a host of business news and data products.

Then there are magazine-based companies such as Time Warner, with its *Fortune*, *Money*, and CNNMoney brands, and a big player on the Web. There's *Forbes* and there was Condé Nast's *Portfolio*, the business magazine whose short life was ended by the recession. These companies don't pretend to have their own staffs covering the world. They pick their spots and aggregate the bigger worldwide business news flow.

Those are just the Old Media companies. Joining them are the new business aggregators, Yahoo Finance, MSN Money Central, Google Finance, and AOL Finance. Yes, the colonizers are busy here as well, and they take in at least 40 percent of online revenue in the business news category.

We also see lots of niches within the business niche—as we do in all niches. Business-to-business, tech, gadget, stocks, and lots more. A sampling of these brands: AllThingsD (owned by News Corporation), TechCrunch, SeekingAlpha, and paidContent (owned by *The Guardian*). (See "Q & A: Rafat Ali," page 150.)

Not to be forgotten are the local niche players, best represented by American City Business Journals and Dolan Media. They cater to highly knowledgeable local business audiences. Though their readerships are small, in the five-digit range in most metro areas, their target demographics are very desirable and increasingly well used by business-oriented advertisers online.

The journalism approach here may be key. "Weeklies are doing it right," says Chris Roush, who runs TalkingBizNews.com, a blog covering the sector. "The average metro daily will do 95 percent of its stories about publicly traded companies—which are 1 percent of the companies out there." That gives the weeklies a lot of firms—big privately held companies and all small businesses—to report on that would otherwise be uncovered.

Just as Seattle is a leader in the diversity of its local sites, it may also offer a lesson about the migration of daily journalists to niches. The *Seattle Post-Intelligencer* had distinguished itself with two business blogs. John Cook's Venture (Capital) Blog and Todd Bishop's Microsoft Blog became must-reading within those communities. Then about a year before the *P-I* closed its print doors and skinnied down to online-only, both jumped ship. They created online TechFlash, in partnership with *Puget Sound Business Journal*, one of the forty regional properties owned by American City Business Journals.

These business blogs and hundreds of other well-written ones around the country point to another way the Web is transforming journalism. Critics have often compared local newspaper sports sections—in which (largely male) readers are assumed to know lots about the teams and leagues—to business sections that are often "dumbed down" to a lowest common denominator. Blogs allow knowledgeable commentators to go deep, satisfying niche audiences, like Microsoft watchers, who have good familiarity with the subject matter.

Digital business journalism in particular has started distinguishing itself through the economic meltdown. Here we've seen much more explanatory journalism—when it was greatly needed. NPR's Adam Davidson created one of the standout business pieces of the times. "The Giant Pool of Money" aired on Ira Glass's *This American Life*, in May 2008 and won a Peabody, broadcasting's highest award. I remember listening to it when it first aired. It was jaw-dropping in its revelation and accessibility, explaining what no one could quite understand: how some bad real estate loans could lead to worldwide global catastrophe. It followed the money in a way no one else had. It had also dropped what Davidson considers a dated form of business journalism. "I feel like the voice of business journalism is sort of, it's an authoritative voice of God," he said. "But there is no authority. It's a process."

Davidson is now part of the new NPR *Planet Money* show, weekly and by podcast. It joins an increasingly crowded group of similar shows, Marketplace's various iterations, of course, and Slate's The Big Money, a business Web site and podcast. There, business editor Jim Ledbetter, and business writers Daniel Gross and Farhad Monjoo serve up a similar fare of smart business journalism for people who may not be in business. Smart explanatory reporting and business blogging are just a couple of the strategies business news players are using.

All of these companies' approaches are remarkably similar, and maybe that's why they've had a hard time busting free of the pack. Their strategies begin with hard news—get it first, get it right, get it out—and then work their way through the laws in Newsonomics: Create multimedia, aggregate, blog, master the technology, and market virally.

It's another spin on how the Digital Dozen are blurring in the text, video, and audio they produce; we're now seeing business news radio programs (with Web sites and podcasts) and business news Web sites (with audio and video).

On the Web, niches take almost infinite—and sometimes surprising—form. Take motherhood. Young mothers have been trading tips and travails for most of human history. They meet in parks and homes for both kids' playtime and a chance to talk to other adults during the day. Now they are doing a lot of meeting online. In all, there are probably more than a hundred local moms' sites across the United States. Gannett is the leader here, making the moms market its first big niche play. MomsLikeMe.com started small, at sites in Indianapolis and Cincinnati, and has gone national, in more than seventy-five cities. Though it's the biggest news company in the country, Gannett decided that these sites were not mainly about news; they were about connecting. So blogging, shared calendars, events, and tips dominate the site, with a little relevant news tossed in. Gannett has put all the sites on a single technology platform, so content and advertising can be shared. Also in the hunt: *The Boston Globe* (BoMoms), *The Orange County Register* (OCMoms) and The Today's Mama chain of more than twenty sites. There are also many independents. When the late NPR newsmagazine *Day to Day* closed shop last year, cohost Madeleine Brand got into the mom's blog and podcast market as well.

Moms sites are classic niche. They take advantage of a life-stage market, and it's one in which people spend a lot of money.

Gannett's parallel niche launch: HighSchoolSports.com. Newspaper companies had long talked about how they "owned" the high school "prep sports" market in print. HighSchoolSports.com aims to capture that young audience. It has similar tools (blogging, calendar, photos, multimedia) and similar niche philosophy: connection.

The evolving Gannett creed: Go after small slices of people with small slices of content.

And now, let's come full circle. If general news, mass news, is a commodity, seemingly all around us, and shunned by advertisers, how do you reinvent it?

Politico has come up with one answer for that: It's not news. It's politics.

Launched three years ago by veterans of *Time* magazine and *The Washington Post*, Politico has rocketed out of literally nowhere to share equal billing with the *Post* and the *Times* on cable talkfests. I'll explore its skillful use of promotion in chapter 10, "Media Learn How to Market, Marketers Find New Ways to Make the Most of Media."

Politico has built a newsroom of more than sixty at this time of great retrenchment elsewhere. How? It is acutely focused on the passion of those in and those who follow politics. Though it seems like an online sensation, most of its revenue still comes from mostly daily papers distributed in and around Capitol Hill. Online, it is able to draw niche-like rates, closer to areas like health and travel than lowly general news.

If Politico has redefined political news, GlobalPost is redefining international news as niche. Started in 2008 by veteran cable news exec Phil Balboni and longtime *Boston Globe* foreign correspondent Charlie Sennott, the site did the unthinkable: paying stipends to more than seventy journalists around the world, each covering a single country. In addition, GlobalPost taps strongly into the Pro-Am model, incorporating the work of more than three thousand bloggers in more than forty nations. I've called Phil Balboni (see "Q & A," below) the Henry Luce of his age because, like Luce, who launched *Fortune* magazine in the teeth of the Great Depression, Balboni launched his enterprise in hard times.

GlobalPost takes international reporting seriously, again at a time when the number of "foreign correspondents" has been cut back dramatically by news and broadcast companies. Balboni and Sennott's article of faith: There is a large enough niche of those hungry for on-the-ground global news, and somehow they'll make a business out of it.

Niches require slicing and dicing. Sometimes the data-centric analysis required to find the target audience. Sometimes, it is in delivering the content to that audience. Both require technology. Let's move on to the next chapter to see how technology is remaking the news.

Q & A: Phil Balboni

Phil Balboni launched GlobalPost in January 2009, just as many news companies were further reducing international reporting. He acted on a forty-year-old idea he'd had about bringing back global news to American audiences—and had seen that the ability of Internet efficiencies now made it possible. GlobalPost is his second career; he founded and ran the award-winning New England Cable News (NECN) business for many years. Now he can look out on the harbor, where clipper ships came in, and beyond, to his growing network of more than seventy correspondents working around the world.

Q: How did your cable news experience inform your GlobalPost plan?

A: There are quite a few, seminal lessons learned from NECN. First, the enormous value of more than one revenue stream and not being solely dependent on advertising.

The most important thing I did on the business side of NECN was throw myself totally into building distribution and selling the network to cable systems—always for cash and never for free. This generated over time enormous growth in steady, reliable revenue that was recession proof and not subject to the ups and downs of the ad market. In my final year, thanks to new contracts with new distributors like Verizon, we were headed toward a double-digit net revenue increase from license fees. Second, the essentiality of intelligent cost control.

Finally, quality works. In journalism, this is generally not believed and, therefore, virtually all media companies chase the largest audience with the lowest common denominator content. We started with a determination to be the high-quality provider of local news on television in New England. We also knew that we would never be the most viewed station with the highest ratings. We created our entire operation and our entire business to be able to be successful as a high-quality provider of content and to live happily with the smaller number of people who wanted an intelligent news product.

Q: What's the moment when the lightbulb went on on how dramatically this new digital business of journalism would be radically different from legacy media?

A: For me, it was probably the fall of 1997, when we launched necn.com as the first all-video-news Web site—perhaps in the world, certainly in the United States. There were probably not more than a couple of dozen broadband connections in the Boston metro area, but we believed in the promise of digital, of being interactive, of letting people have what they wanted in the order they wanted it, and only what they wanted.

And then I saw how slowly this built, how long it took for people to catch on to the power of the Web to deliver video, but we never doubted that we were doing the right thing, and today the power of video has swept over the Internet.

Q: What have you learned about the role—and economics—of bloggers that surprised you?

A: I am constantly amazed at the enormous scope of blogging and the immediacy of its viral power. I would never have expected it to have come this far but it has, and shows no signs of any significant slowdown. To the contrary, the economics are generally not there, and blogging is not of great interest to advertisers. There are certainly some exceptions, but I don't see this changing much. It is more of a social networking and intellectual engagement tool than an economic one.

Q: Is this "freelance stipend" model a big part of journalism's future?

A: I do believe that it will be a meaningful part of the future for journalists as the large and well-endowed media companies disassemble. It puts the burden on the journalist to cobble together the means of his or her support, but, on the other hand, it offers more freedom, more flexibility, and more creativity than being yoked to one entity. We do hope, and expect, to reward the best of our correspondents with compensation that will look more and more like full-time payment. That depends on our overall economics, of course, but it is part of the game plan for GlobalPost.

Q & A: Rafat Ali

RAFAT ALI *is founder, publisher and editor of ContentNext Media. Reuters described its success well: "ContentNext's flagship paidContent, founded in 2002, has quickly established itself as a must-read among executives in the media and digital media sector." PaidContent has indeed been a daily stop for those involved in the business of news, media, and entertainment industries. In addition, the company runs parallel sites for the United Kingdom and India and around mobile content.*

Q: PaidContent filled a niche no one had previously seen as clearly as you did. How did you see the niche, define it, and make sure you got it as focused as you could?

A: This was the depths of Internet recession in 2002 in New York City, and I was looking for a way to raise my profile, and this seemed like a good way to showcase my skills as an online journalist covering online media and the Internet. I was aiming for a new job with the likes of *WSJ* and CNET then. Of course, no one was hiring in those days, much less hiring an online journalist covering online media.

I was working for what then was Silicon Alley Daily, the online and e-mail remnant of the magazine *Silicon Alley Reporter*. I joined it right after the print magazine closed, and online and the e-mail newsletter remained. There, after a few months of working, I was the last man standing, sort of, as the company started to lay off other journalists, and I learned to do a lot more with a lot less, including editing my own stories.

The daily coverage meant I saw the trend: Online advertising had tanked, and a definite trend toward premium and subscription content online, with sites such as NYTimes.com, TheStreet.com, Salon.com and others experimenting with it. The idea—even then—was that this wasn't the only way in a downturn, but that it was essential to experiment with all sorts of revenue models, and having multiple legs meant overall some would work better than others as economic cycles came through.

As the economy came back, so did advertising online, and the paid content trend went on the backburner for most of the online publishers. The key for us was focus: covering the money flow for online media, where it went in and how it came out. As long as we were at the intersection of technology and how it affected the business models and financing of digital media, we were safe as a viable business. PaidContent began covering all the ways in which content gets paid for, and covering it across all sectors and geographies. That also meant defining "content" in as broad a manner as possible, across tradition and new media, entertainment and information sectors, with the focus being on content aimed at and generated by individual consumers.

Q: You've combined business coverage of entertainment and journalism businesses. What major idea should news publishers take away about the relevance of the entertainment business to their own business models?

A: Entertainment was the lowest-hanging fruit, and the first to be affected by the changes in digital media, as consumer consumption patterns changed. I saw and covered firsthand the decimation of the music industry with the advent of Napster and realized that this was going to happen to the news business very soon. Both these legacy businesses were built on the economics of scarcity, something that digital media did away with. Also, packaging as defined top-down didn't matter anymore in entertainment, as the remix culture took hold, and the same became true very soon for the journalism and news businesses as well. What is different is that great investigative journalism has a lot more civic value than great entertainment, and funding that requires a lot more creativity than publishers have displayed till now.

Q: What's the moment when the lightbulb went on on how the economics of this new digital business would be radically different from legacy publishing?

A: It would be clichéd to say it was the advent of blogging, but, for me, it was when Blogger.com launched in the late nineties. That showed how easy it was to publish, and how it could be used to deliver news, opinion, and aggregation in a very efficient way. Also, a few years later, it was the advent of RSS feeds and newsreaders, and how news packaging as defined by publishers went away. It really defined how personalized interest areas defined by users would be the way going forward. Monetizing this age of dispersed media was very different, and was on a very different scale and margins, than legacy. The cost of experimenting with any of these innovations came down dramatically, and publishers had to learn how to do a lot more with a lot less, and at the same time, competing with a lot more sources online.

Q: What lesson in digital publishing do you wish you'd learned faster?

A: I underestimated the value of comments when I was building the business, back in 2002–2003, and adding community later became a lot more difficult for us down the line. For us, it was about giving the news as accurately and efficiently as we could, and my contention was that our expert readers could form their own conclusions and opinions on it. We did have pithy analysis and opinion occasionally, and continue to have it, but later on we learned that a heavy mix of all of it is what the users wanted. In some senses, we were top-down too, and that we should have rectified sooner. Also, blogging in a specific trade vertical means you will hit a scaling issue (getting big enough, fast enough) sooner or later, and that means building replicable models in other verticals (content niches) too. We also should have learned that lesson sooner.

Q & A: Nancy Shute

NANCY SHUTE, *a twenty-year veteran of* U.S. News & World Report, *has covered science and medicine for national publications for more than twenty years. Many of us focus on national news, local news, economic news, and the like, but science news greatly impacts our lives. It, too, is suffering in the news traumas we're seeing.*

Usha McFarling, a science journalist who won a 2007 Pulitzer Prize for explanatory writing, argues that "media atrophy" is reducing the discourse on vital issues—at the worst possible time. In her reportage on climate change she showed how vested interests (from both the right and the left side) "hijacked" the story to fit their agendas, but not serve the public overall.

Nancy Shute is familiar with these issues. She has produced multimedia packages and has been a guest on NPR, CNN, CBS, NBC, WETA, and WTOP. Now she serves as a contributing editor for U.S. News & World Report, *where she writes the OnParenting blog.*

Q: For science and medical journalists, what new opportunities has the Web opened up?

A: The Web has transformed science and medical journalism. Just ten years ago we followed the major medical journals by waiting for copies to plop into the mailbox. Now we follow global efforts to quell the 2009 swine flu outbreak on e-mail networks like ProMed, as well as the Centers for Disease Control's emergency Twitter feed, dozens of blogs written by epidemiologists and physicians, and streaming video from Health and Human Services.

Medical information has become much more accessible, thanks to open-access journals and large online databases such as those at the National Library of Medicine. I can find patients to interview on Facebook and other social networking sites. Science and medical writers are also much better connected to each other thanks to social networking sites like Facebook and Twitter, which should help improve the quality and accuracy of our work. It's certainly making our daily life a lot more collegial, and fun.

Q: Are we entering into a new gig economy for journalists, in which they have to piece together a number of jobs, rather than shooting for one and holding on to it?

A: Many science writers already have entered the gig economy, a trend that started well before our current media meltdown. In the early 1980s, the membership of the National Association of Science Writers was dominated by staff writers for newspapers and news-weeklies. Now two-thirds of NASW members say they're freelancers. Many of those independent journalists are doing very well, with clients in multiple sectors, including corporate, nonprofit, and academia, not just general-interest publishing.

Many are self-publishing with their own Web sites or blogs. I've joined the gig economy, too. After twelve years at *U.S. News & World Report* as both a senior writer and assistant managing editor in charge of the magazine's science and technology coverage, I'm stitching together gigs that include blogging for *U.S. News*, freelancing for some print publications, teaching journalism and science writing, and testing business models for a health news start-up.

Q: What do you tell young journalists about the trade they are now getting into?

A: What a fabulous time to get into journalism! You'll be building the future of our trade! It's like *All the President's Men*, *High School Musical*, and the founding days of Google all rolled into one. And if you just don't have the stomach for a start-up, that's fine, too. There are still jobs out there for good writers, editors, and designers, and many of them are for print publications. We readers still need you.

Q: What lesson in digital media do you wish you'd learned faster?

A: I wish I'd made myself learn one new digital skill a month, even if it was just a tiny one like cropping in PhotoShop. Since the skills and tools are constantly evolving, the old "next year I'll learn Audacity" approach just doesn't cut it; it's too easy to let my awareness of new tools slide, and then feel overwhelmed. Having said that, I'd better step up. This weekend, I vow to build a new Web site using WordPress!

9

Apply the 10 Percent Rule

We often get blinded by the forms in which content is produced, rather than the job that the content does. —**TIM O'REILLY, Internet pioneer**

If you do build a great experience, customers tell each other about that. Word of mouth is very powerful. —**JEFF BEZOS, Amazon founder**

Driving into the YahooPlex in Sunnyvale, you remember the devil-may-care Yahoo commercials. You know, the ones that ended with the endless, semi-yodeled "Yahooooooooooooo!" Maybe, it's the big, kind-of-goofy purple and yellow logo, jauntily off kilter. "On campus," there's still the Silicon Valley workplace air, casual to the max, lots of good food choices and free barista-made drinks.

CEO Carol Bartz now has ridden into town, bringing a new intention of order—never Yahoo's strong suit—and accountability. The company has seen roller-coaster change since its 1995 founding, and it has been battered in comparison to its little brother, who got famously rich and better-looking, Google, headquartered just miles away in Mountain View.

Yahoo, though, still produces more than $7 billion in revenue a year. Astoundingly, it reaches 562.6 million individuals a month. That's more than half the world's population that's online. The secret of the success is neither content nor advertising. Its secret is technology.

Yahoo was born a technology company, and that's the basis of all that it does. In the digital world, technology makes or breaks ideas. It also provides the foundation for all the laws cited in this book.

Both the digital reader and ad revolutions that have transformed the news business have been driven by technologies that removed old barriers of space and time. Aggregation couldn't happen without the organizational abilities of the technologies. New content creation from online multimedia, blogging, and all the user-generated stuff derive from our new abilities to create on computer screens. Niching is a sorting-on-steroids that could only be laboriously done by hand not long ago.

Technology not only makes some things possible that weren't, but it makes most everything to do with the news business easier and faster. It's a multiplier and enabler of human effort. So I call Law No. 9: Apply the 10 Percent Rule. The idea: At this stage of digital evolution, we should be beyond the man versus machine debate and value each for what it contributes. Google has proudly noted that its Google News product is free of the taint of human judgment. No pesky editors. It's all based on The Algorithm, how Google decides which search results to show us in what order. On the other end of the old argument are newsroom types, who believe it's all about human judgment, about the editorial-intensive weighing of quality.

Clearly, we're at a point where we can better understand how the machines and people fit together. I'm no technology expert, but I've come to see the fundamental value contributed by databases, algorithms, metrics, and content-creation software. In talking with many technology companies and the publishers they serve, I've come to the 10 Percent Rule.

Let technology do as much of the heavy lifting as possible—that's the 90 percent—and let humans come along and work on top of the technology, adding the skills, the intelligence, and the judgment. It's that 10 percent that will differentiate what the technology can do. Sometimes it's a "presentation layer"; that's the face of the news and information. Sometimes it's the weighing, understanding the bigness of a story to an audience, the kind of packaging experienced editors are often so good at. Sometimes it is looking at the run of stories the technology is surfacing and making greater sense of them—seeing a bigger story in the story and then creating it.

We're very much at the beginning here, too, of figuring out this machine-human equation, how much, when, why, and how. It certainly isn't a hard 90-10 rule, and will vary by technology, by company, and by product.

Yet look at what the impact of news technologies has been so far:

CONSIDER:

- Ad targeting: As we've seen, this is the biggest driver of change in the news industry. Paid-search advertising dominates the $23 billion online ad industry in the United States and worldwide. Almost half that spending goes to paid search, with Google dominating that category. Paid search is all about matching ad messages to content—reading the content for clues that suggest which ads to serve.

  Classifieds (14 percent) are the third biggest category (after the less-targeted banner ads), and these, of course, are all driven by database-matching technologies as well. Online classifieds do what the browsable print ones could never do—find matching pins in the two haystacks of employers' job openings and job seekers' skills, for instance. Lead generation (7 percent), of course, depends on technologies identifying likely sales prospects.

  In the multinodal world of digital advertising, ad-targeting technologies are now used by a wide range of players, from digital ad agencies to thousands of ad networks and exchanges to media companies. In turn, all Internet ad revenue, of course, is dependent on numerous systems of tech-based creation, hosting, distribution, and payment systems.

- A number of the Q & A contributors to this book have said that search engine optimization has offered them their biggest lesson in the Web business. Or "findability" as Chuck Richard puts it (see "Q & A," page 165). Simply, publishing isn't good enough. The huge search-engine optimization business performs like a talent agent in the old world who grabbed the bullhorn and touted his client's talents. Here, though, the bullhorn is the deep and evolving understanding of how Google and the other big search engines "read" content and "optimize" it so it can be found—and can then be placed on top of the other guy's content. It's an unseen war being fought 24/7 behind your desktop.

- Content management systems (or CMSs) have transformed the creation of online journalism, though most Old Media still have to maintain two technology systems, one for the old, one for the new. (See "Newsonomics 101: What the Newspaper and Post Office Have in Common," page 162.) John Girard, another Stanford grad (like the Yahoo and Google founders), created Clickability, an early Web-only CMS for news publishers, in 1999. The tech-based, news-focused CMS company continues to change with the times. For news publishers like Wendy Warren (see "Q & A," page 69) at Philly.com, the Clickability CMS is the basis for most of what it publishes: the news, the blogs, the community-created content, the multimedia, the events, and more. At the Web's beginning, online news operations had to spend a lot of time on processing. Now the technology—Clickability's and many free, open-source solutions as well as bigger, corporate ones—has matured, and news professionals can concentrate on the audience experience, leaving the grunt work to technology.

- Metrics are transforming the news trade. Fifteen years ago, many newspaper companies didn't even know the names of their home delivery subscribers; they only kept the addresses on clipboards! Now news companies are joining the modern business world. Of course, customer relationship management (CRM) software is a must; you have to know and track customers—and would-be ones. Metrics, though, cover the waterfront, telling publishers exactly who is using what, or not using it, on their sites. Staff bloggers regularly check their relative standing. Yes, we could fall into a journalism-by-the-numbers business if good judgment isn't applied, but there's no turning back on what people in the business of news can now know—instantly—about what's making a difference and what's not.

- Data mining sounds like an old trade updated. It is. What's in the mine here, though, is the almost infinite volume of content that has been created—think rich and increasingly digitized archives— and is being created as we speak. Technology companies like Montreal-based Nstein and Aggregate Knowledge (see "Q & A, Paul Martino," page 168) are among the many new miners; they provide the computer linguistics that enable the user to read all the content in any publisher's vat and interrelate it by topic, source, geography, and more. Data mining will have a huge impact on the news products that will be created and, when connected to ad targeting, how new money will be made.
- Technology helps publishers manage audiences more flexibly than was ever before possible. *The Wall Street Journal*'s online subscription revenue approaches $100 million a year, but accounts for only a million of its unique visitors. It manages its other 20 million monthly visitors through sophisticated slicing and dicing of its content niches and the differing access points and levels it allows differing audiences.
- Publishers are getting smarter about content, improving what I call their content IQ. That means knowing what they produce intimately—by topic, by niche, by location, by audience and advertiser interest, and more. The higher the content IQ, the better publishers can control how they play the game of online content.
- Coming: We'll soon see a new round of technologies applied to personalizing the news-reading experience; many companies are working to find that Holy Grail.

We could go on and on with technologies that are transforming the news trade, as dizzying as it can be. But you don't have to be a technologist to understand the basic impact. You just come back to readers and viewers on the one hand—the audience—and merchants on the other. Much of the activity is about that simple activity of matching—better and better and better—those two.

It's not just happening with words on paper or pixel. Online ad pioneer Dave Morgan (see "Q & A," page 167) is off on still another start-up, Simulmedia. It focuses on the TV world. He says, "Our goal will be to use sophisticated data analysis and predictive technology to redirect where and when cable operators and broadcast and cable networks place these [ad] spots in order to make them more effective and efficient in delivering the most desirable audiences." There you go.

Take just one editorial product I've mentioned, the Times Extra service of NYTimes.com. (See "Q & A: Marc Frons," page 170.) Times Extra provides "contextual links" to stories from news sources other than the *Times*, right there in little green type on the *Times*'s home page. Times Extra is powered by Blogrunner, a company the *Times* bought. Basically, all those choices of which stories to pick up—based on which key words from which sources—are made by the Blogrunner technology. Humans—editors—can make changes in the algorithm, in key words and sources, of course, and that's 10 percent of the work, the human judgment applied in getting a result for readers that makes the most sense. Where do they make those changes? In the algorithm, of course.

Ah, the algorithm. It's the word that technology people often used in the last decade to shut up the content people. As in, "Don't you understand? It's in the algorithm." Long story short: Algorithms are basically sets of instructions that tell the technology how to operate. That hugely influential Google search algorithm—its secret blend of linking, relevance, and recency—is endlessly being tweaked to improve results, and then divined by the search engine-optimization people. Algorithms tell technology how to be deployed; they do 90 percent of the work. The 10 percent should be the humans telling the algorithms how to work.

On the creation end of the news business, technology just makes things easier. First off, there's no longer a single deadline. "You can publish when you are ready to publish, not when the presses roll," says New West's Jonathan Weber. Technology "has made the publishing process much more efficient. You can access a wide range of sources so easily."

For working journalists (and analysts), technology is a multiplier. We can research, interview, write, edit, tweak, customize, and distribute at light-speed compared to the old days of Smith-Corona typewriters, reporter's notebooks, teletypes, and endless galleys of corrections.

Let's consider one other news-related industry, in which technology has completely transformed the business. It's the business of media monitoring. That's a little industry that serves companies concerned about what is said about them in the press. Just after the turn of the millennium, I had the opportunity to visit BurrellesLuce, a company that's long been a leader in media monitoring.

Down one corridor, I could see how the business has been done since the 1930s. Literally, older editors wearing green eyeshades and wielding scissors cut out articles from newspapers and magazines. These articles are then collected, put in a folder, and mailed off to the companies buying the "monitoring" service or to their public relations people.

Down another corridor, Art Wynne III, the grandson of the firm's founder, showed me the future. It was a scanner. The scanner replaces the old manual process and the software follows, sorting individual articles, bylines, publication names, and more.

This was a business literally transitioning centuries, within one building. (See below.)

NEWSONOMICS 101: What the Newspaper and Post Office Have in Common

Our news confusion in this Hybrid Age has a parallel in another business about as storied in American history as the newspaper. In this case, as in newspapers, we see how the technology, or the lack of it, slowly dooms a good practice to oblivion.

Consider the post office. Last year, the U.S. Postal Service got still another rate increase, leading many Americans to believe that the Forever stamp was becoming the best thing in their portfolios. At the same time, the USPS talked about eliminating Saturday delivery, saying it couldn't afford it. Those twin moves prompted a few outcries and queries about the place of the USPS in the country today.

Should we taxpayers further subsidize mail delivery, all to serve the couple-of-centuries-old notion that universal mail delivery (read delivery to every nook and cranny of the far-flung

(continued)

---

nation) when, on a parallel track, the feds are putting $6 billion into bringing broadband access to . . . the farther reaches of the nation?

The goals of ancient post office delivery and of broadband extension are the same: equalizing basic communication services for all Americans, no matter where they live.

We can see the collision of the eighteenth and twenty-first centuries here.

In this hybrid, where-the-hell-are-we stage, we are planning on paying for two ways to make sure everyone stays in touch. Both are expensive, but one we can bet will be needed in ten years and the other . . . not so much.

It's curiously similar to the hybrid tortures endured by newspaper companies. They must keep the pulp-and-ink processing behemoths oiled and delivery trucks gassed up just to hold on to the Sunday circulars and remaining classifieds. Yet they must invest in online, a clearly superior (timely, environmental, cheaper) way to deliver the news. They want to get out of the old business, in which technology provides no 10 percent solution, but can't afford to.

It's no coincidence that as the post office pondered dropping Saturday delivery, newspapers started doing the same thing.

Flash forward to the election of 2008.

No one could wait for a mailed packet of articles; the idea would seem absurd. Politicians turned to Critical Mention, a New York start-up headed by serial entrepreneur Sean Morgan. For Barack Obama, Hillary Clinton, John McCain, Mitt Romney, and the others, Critical Mention's assemblage of video-recording devices and proprietary software scanned broadcasts and cablecasts around the world. Not once a day, or even once an hour. Every six seconds.

Critical Mention didn't just scan the usual suspects, ABC, CBS, CNN, and so. It scanned news broadcasters around the world, including five Arabic-language news networks!

Then those politicians and their operatives, logging into a password-protected site, could see exactly what was being said about them by whom, around the clock.

Of course, politicians aren't the only ones to find the service useful. Federal security services and Fortune 500 companies use it as well.

Again, at least 90 percent of the work is done by the technology. Remember all those green eyeshade people of another generation? Well, their "editor" jobs have been replaced by IT jobs of various kinds. It's a new world, far from the old newspaper work.

In the eighties in Saint Paul, I remember the daily negotiation with Jack Hickey to get a bit more space for stories and photos in this section or that. Jack, a longtime production department veteran of the *Pioneer Press*, drew the next day's pages, the "news hole" for stories and space for ads. He did it for years, by hand, with a pencil. If a big story broke, I had to call him and cajole him for space. He'd oblige whenever he could, but rarely without a big sigh, for a change meant a lot of new pencil-and-eraser work for him. In fact, I also remember how the paper counted its ad linage. For years, a Finance Department employee used a ruler, page by page, to count the inch dimensions of each ad, and then total it up. I think that job got replaced by technology awhile back.

Technology has been a huge disrupter of business as usual. Yet, harnessed properly, it can be a boon; it can do a lot of the drudgery that long has been part of the trade.

Let's recall the 1936 Charlie Chaplin masterpiece, *Modern Times*. Its iconic photo is Chaplin spread-eagled on the massive gears and pulleys of the then-emerging Industrial Age. Charlie was its victim, a pawn of the Big Machine. For news people fully entering the Digital News Decade, the goal is to have a hand on the levers of the new digital machines, so that they don't end up, Tramp-like, subject to the whims of others.

One of the many established trades that the new technologies are changing is marketing. In our next chapter, let's look at how new marketing is changing how news gets sold and how marketers are trying to make sense of this new digital news world.

Q & A: Chuck Richard

CHUCK RICHARD serves as a vice president and an analyst colleague of mine at Outsell. He's one of my top go-to people on anything having to do with advertising spending, lead generation, and business-to-business (B2B) trade publishing and company information, including vertical search. His executive-level consulting is highly valued, even by Yankee fans, though his Red Sox colors can't help but show through.

Chuck's not only a fan, but a keen observer of one the most successful paid consumer content services in the country, Major League Baseball's MLB.com.

Q: What is it about MLB that's made it such a successful paid-content product?

I've used MLB since the late 1990s and routinely call it the best service, period, on the Web. Way ahead of the Web strategists' and analysts' exhortations, MLB.com launched, right out of the box, the perfect work-flow solution for baseball fans. Of course, it's "fun flow" or "leisure flow," but based on the same principles.

To access a very deep, many-many-dimensional database, I don't need to learn an interface, I just need to click on a box score. To follow a game live I don't need to learn hot keys, I just look at a baseball field that is full of metadata, accessible by clicking on the pitcher for pitch count and balls and strikes, on a batter's name for all his stats, and a real-time K-Zone showing the trajectory of each pitch, its speed, and location at the plate.

And although I have lived only five years of my sixty-one years in the city of my beloved Red Sox, I listen to most games on MLB.com with its live audio feeds of every game, every night, and have a choice of the home team or visiting team announcers. The fee for this feature is $14.95, a price that has increased only slowly from the first year, back in the nineties, when I started subscribing.

A: The ultimate expression of the success of MLB.com was a decision by the thirty major-league teams to scuttle a proposed public offering of MLB Advanced Media some years ago. The owners each contributed $1 million to set up the League's interactive unit,

$30 million total start-up capital, with the understanding they would contribute additional $1 million tranches each. But MLB.com was so successful that they never needed to ask for any additional rounds. This success fueled IPO fever, but the owners nixed it when they realized the public disclosure requirements would reveal just how profitable MLB.com was and the players union would demand a share of it!

Q: What are the top skills journalists need in the new gig economy, in which journalists have to piece together a number of jobs, rather than shooting for one and holding on to it?

A: As an undergraduate English major, high school English teacher, one-time aspiring writer, and now, as an analyst, a specialized type of professional writer, it pains me to highlight what is making Demand Media, Huffington Post, AllBusiness, About.com, and similar companies so successful: analytics-wired editorial.

DemandMedia explains the new content mantra succinctly: Findability (having your content found by search engines) is paramount, and quality has nothing to do with findability. They add, engagement, return visits, and loyalty absolutely depend on some form of quality, or at least some "hook."

As someone who loves language, in all its forms, from the radio addresses of Winston Churchill, the genius meanderings of Laurence Stern in *Tristram Shandy*, to Walt Kelly's skewering of McCarthyism in his syndicated *Pogo* strips, it pains me to highlight the ascendancy of analytics over language and great content. But this is the key skill, or realization, for journalists: Keep your love of journalism and writing, but learn that it's only the stories that find the right audiences at the right time and therefore attract unique visitors and ad dollars that will keep your employers afloat.

Q: What do you tell young journalists about the trade they are now getting into?

A: You are entering the profession at the end of the first stage of a six-hundred-year-old revolution! The only thing certain is that every tried-and-true rule, every best practice, and every bit of conventional wisdom has been devalued. But be absolutely certain that the current

ugly and ungainly mess of Google News, blogs, Tweets, citizen journalists, mobile Web, wireless networks, cellular accessibility, and
multimedia extravaganzas is totally transitory.

This is 100 percent certainly not the end game; it's just the first
new atmosphere that has rushed in to fill the vacuum left when the
old print-on-paper model succumbed.

Rather than shying away from the profession, rush toward it and
be a part of the excitement of shaping and maybe leading the second,
third, and fourth stages that are yet to play out.

So, if your model of journalism is being the next Edward R. Mur-
row or even Maureen Dowd, you're in for a disappointment. But if,
instead, your eyes widen and your pulse quickens with excitement
about wading into the free-for-all, you're headed in the right direction.

Q: What can those in the news trade—journalists and business
managers—learn from B2B digital transition experience?

A: In everyday conversation, when B2B trade publishing professionals routinely speak of their customers, they mean their advertisers. An apocryphal, but telling, story is that B2B trade publishers put
articles in their magazines "to keep the ads from sticking together."

What's key about these stories is that B2B trade publishing has
always "followed the money" first and the reader second. By con-
trast, news publishers and newspaper journalists have always followed the story and the reader first. This segment has done a good
job of quickly adapting to the opportunities for lead generation that
combine extremely relevant content with advertisers and suppliers
of goods and services exactly matched to that content.

Q & A: Dave Morgan

DAVE MORGAN *is one of the Web's great advertising pioneers.*

*A serial entrepreneur, Morgan previously founded and ran both
TACODA, Inc., an online advertising company that pioneered behavioral online marketing and was acquired by AOL in 2007 for
$275 million, and Real Media, Inc., one of the world's first ad serv-
ing and online ad network companies and a predecessor to 24/7 Real*

Media (TFSM), which was later sold to WPP for $649 million. Then he spent a little time as executive vice president for Global Advertising Strategy, at AOL. He's now CEO of New York City–based Simulmedia, Inc., a TV-facing tech start-up.

Q: When you find a likable, talkative seatmate on an airline, how do you explain to them the impact of predictive technology?

A: Disruptive technologies act like water, eroding artificial barriers in markets and businesses that don't add maximum value to their customers. They tend to short-circuit market participants that get too fat, arrogant, and lazy—not unlike what networked digital communications technologies are doing to the newspaper industry.

Q: You have deep experience in behavioral targeting. How soon will it be when the news we read will be agreeably determined by watching our clickstream/search history/buying patterns?

A: I expect that within five years consumers will see a significant improvement in the personal relevance of most of the news, entertainment, and information that they receive, particularly commercial communication.

Q: What's not on publishers' radar screens that should be?

A: Publishers need to wake up to the fact that consumers don't need them. They need content producers and curators, and the platforms to access them, but not packagers and distributors for much longer.

Q: What lesson in digital media do you wish you'd learned faster?

A: Align your interests with consumers and those disrupting markets, rather than trying to help legacy players defend their turf. You never really win fighting the inevitable, unless, of course, you are a consultant and just want the short-term fee revenue.

Q & A: Paul Martino

PAUL MARTINO is the CEO and cofounder of Aggregate Knowledge, the fourth company that he has founded over his twenty-year tech-

nology career. One of those companies was early social site Tribe Network, which was acquired by Cisco. Aggregate Knowledge is a hypermarketing "discovery" company, aiming to present one-to-one delivery of both news content and advertising through extensive use of data and technology.

Q: What big truths do most publishers miss in thinking about digital content, as compared to print content?

A: Readers are king, and static content is dead. We've found that the more publishers let their readers drive the content, and the more the content changes as a result of relevancy, the greater the engagement, immersion, and return visits. This is now a growing phenomenon, thanks to reviews, comments, blogs, and "discovery" windows—those windows that say "People who read this also read . . ." Forward-thinking publishers are turning their millions of readers into editors who are dynamically determining the most relevant and interesting content to recommend to others.

Q: What's the moment you recall when the lightbulb went on of how the economics of this new digital business would be radically different from legacy publishing?

A: It started with Web 2.0 and social networking in the early 2000s. In 2003, when I founded Tribe.net, one of the first social networks, we noticed that people loved to follow what their "friends" were doing, and we also noticed that common interests bonded groups of friends. People started sharing everything and the "wisdom of crowds" surged. This is the same principle around the new economics of news publishing. Let the crowds dictate, in essence, by creating user-driven editorial machines. That translates into deeper engagement, more revenue-generating page views, and higher purchase conversions of "relevant" page ads—also driven by user behavior—and increased return visits.

Q: What's the rough mix and handoff between technology and editorial expertise, given the tools of the day?

A: As editorial expertise continues to shift to the "wisdom of the crowd," the editors must become more and more technologically savvy. A single blogger breaking a news story from his living room is not likely to be guided by significant editorial expertise. He or she is just trying to get the story out. Mastering the now cheap distribution technologies (blogs, YouTube, social networks, etc.) is the key to success. As for getting that specific story noticed and talked about, that's where the editorial expertise is of more importance.

Q: What one big thing that will change their businesses should publishers realize is coming soon?

A: The way advertisements are served—to the individual, not as random opaque inventory. This isn't necessarily [so much] a change just for publishers, as it is a change for advertising in general. Ads will be based on real-time decision engines that track click-stream data, leverage third-party data, and mine contextual data through analytical scans of trillions of data points. Each reader will be shown personalized ads and ad-creatives tailored to that specific reader as a truly one-to-one message. This personalized messaging is the only way to break through the almost complete ad blindness that is now prevalent on the Web as a whole. As the ads get more and more targeted and measurable, the kind of content that attracts a specific audience will get better and better understood. It's at this point that the highest quality and measurable results will be delivered for marketers.

Now, instead of saying, "I want to buy the front page of Yahoo Finance," the marketer will say, "Find me one million people who will be receptive to buying a new housing refinance offer." Therefore, a publisher must focus on delivering high value audiences regardless of the specific content that they might be presenting at any moment.

Q & A: Marc Frons

MARC FRONS oversees technology and product development as chief technology officer, digital operations at NYTimes.com. His tenure has seen a galloping advance in Times *tech initiatives. Before coming to the* Times, *he served as CTO for The Wall Street Journal Online and other Dow Jones consumer Web sites.*

He's a technologist who began his career as a journalist, working at Newsweek *and* Business Week. *He got his start online starting up the financial Web site SmartMoney.com, where he held the unusual title of editor and chief technology officer.*

Q: The NYT iPhone app has been the leading news app. What lessons did you apply to come up with this successful launch?

A: For our iPhone app, we wanted to create an application with production values similar to the iPhone itself. In other words, it had to be extremely easy to use, highly functional, and beautiful. We wanted iPhone users to experience reading the news on a mobile device in a new way, one that took advantage of the graphical possibilities of the iPhone and the ability to read offline, which we saw as a major benefit at the time.

Q: Digital publishing lets technology do a lot of the heavy lifting, with editorial or marketing overlay. Given that change, how do you now explain the new handshake between technology and journalism?

A: With print in obvious and permanent decline, more and more journalists have come to realize that digital is the future, and if they want to have a place in that future, they need to understand technology and the technologist. I think many journalists have come to appreciate the power of technology to help them tell stories in new and compelling ways.

Technology is what makes it possible for journalists in the digital age to connect with readers, to visualize data, to combine video, photography, maps, and other elements in their articles. At the same time, technologists (at least where I work) have become more attuned to the needs of journalists. These days, the best news organizations will be those where journalists understand the capabilities and limitations of technology, and where technologists understand the capabilities and limitations of journalism.

Q: What's the moment when the lightbulb went on on how much this new digital business of journalism would be radically different from legacy publishing?

A: For me, personally, having abandoned print in 1995 to start SmartMoney.com, the lightbulb was seeing Mosaic for the first time a year or two before that. But I don't think I fully appreciated how different print and digital would become until blogs, Google Ad-Words and AdSense created an economy for digital publishing that we had not seen before.

Q: What lesson in digital media do you wish you'd learned faster?

A: All of them, but especially the importance of search and of search-engine optimization. Second, the importance of simplicity, speed, and ease of use; and third, the importance of data (combined with a core set of values) in making decisions.

10

Media Learn How to Market, Marketers Find New Ways to Make the Most of Media

Putting out a newspaper without promotion is like winking at a girl in the dark—well-intentioned, but ineffective.—**WILLIAM RANDOLPH HEARST, publisher**

Give up control and give it away. The more you give your idea away, the more your company is going to be worth.—**SETH GODIN, author**

Here's *Salon*'s editor in chief Joan Walsh at America's best baseball stadium, ATT Park in San Francisco. She has gone down to visit her friend Tony, and the ushers let them move to some empty seats in the first row, right behind home plate. Tony's wife has called to say they are on TV. Then, the horrific play.

Mike Cameron rocketed a line drive off rookie Giants pitcher Joe Martinez's temple. He crumpled to the ground. Astoundingly, a few minutes later, he was able to walk off the field and get to the hospital for the requisite MRIs and CT scans.

The event reminded Joan of the recent demise of actress Natasha Richardson after a skiing accident and of similar head injuries in baseball.

How do I know this?

Joan didn't call me. She blogged it on her "Not just another Joan Walsh blog!" which is related to, but different than, her official Joan Walsh blog on *Salon*. Of course, the blog post wasn't just a blog post. Automatically, through the magic of the Web, it went on to Twitter so that those following Joan could know about the post and click through to it.

For Walsh, modern media is about ubiquity. Sure, she runs *Salon*, and writes her two blogs—one political, the other personal. Through Twitter, you'll see her takes on Joe Biden, Rupert Murdoch, Bruce Springsteen, and, of course, her beloved San Francisco Giants. Tune in Chris Matthews's *Hardball* show on MSNBC, and she'll often occupy one of the talking squares, contributing to the ping-ponged discourse.

Walsh is a modern media figure, understanding that her work and personal life now blend together, and that her profile helps build the business. She's not just a journalistic player; she's a social player.

It used to be simple. Now, though, the new laws of media have greatly confused the worlds of marketing and advertising.

It used to be that if you ran a news media operation, your marketing consisted mainly of publishing or broadcasting a story and figuring the world would notice. Sure, newspapers ran a few "house ads"—in *their own* publications—about upcoming stories or special sections, but they were loath to spend money. Advertising was something they sold, not something they bought! Broadcasters, too, used their own time, sprinkled here and there. Both were used to what we might call silo marketing—letting everyone within your own silo, your current customers, know what was coming.

Marketers, too, knew how to use this relatively stable world of media. They and their public relations companies worked the known, slowly changing landscape. Media monitoring companies compiled, mildly updated, and resold endlessly their lists of media contacts. Those contacts got the press releases and the phone calls. Products and launches were written up and broadcast. Everyone was happy.

Marketing, though, has seen its own parallel revolution to what the news world has experienced. Much of it concerns viral marketing, parallel to the social networking revolution that we're in the midst of, and part of it is simply about old-fashioned, savvy promotion applied across media. Where once great mass markets, served by newspapers and broadcasters, were the easy, standard way to sell products and services, the viral Web is giving both marketers and media headaches and unexpected opportunities.

It's a major transformation in its own right and leads us to Law No. 10: Media Learn How to Market, Marketers Find New Ways to Make the Most of Media.

Consider this new world:

- Most news organizations are embracing social networks less quickly than their readers and viewers. While they've adopted some basics of commenting and blogging, their customers are a-Twitter and dwelling on Facebook.
- The "statusphere" is increasingly where people hang out online. The average time spent on Facebook each month is two hours—and that's about 10 times what an individual spends on a local news Web site.
- The adoption of social networking is generational, but is increasing across the board. The average ages of users of the top four services: Twitter, 31; Facebook, 26; MySpace, 27; and LinkedIn, 40.
- While the Internet has surpassed newspapers in national and international news reading, TV still remains supreme, with 70 percent of Americans saying that's their preferred source. That makes "getting on TV" still a huge promotional goal.

For media and journalists themselves, it has been an intriguing evolution. It is no longer enough just to create good or great work. The always-on, free-for-all Internet world is an echo chamber. It blows out—and sometimes up—the profound and the trivial. In the attention economy, with the gatekeepers on hiatus, it's all about getting your brand, your story, and yourself out there and having others multiply your impact.

Joan Walsh finds that many of her journalistic and media contemporaries are just as connected as she is. On Twitter in a recent month, you can see she is following more than a hundred of them—including Rachel Maddow, Craig Newmark, and Nicholas Kristof—and they've all got their own followers and connections. Such social networks offer a new passport through our lives, and smart media are learning how to use them.

Alan Murray, deputy managing editor at *The Wall Street Journal*, is leading the social media revolution at that paper, which began publishing in 1889 when electricity was first commercially harnessed. He's finding journalists who like to write often and already use social networks. Then he wades into territory that journalists have traditionally considered taboo.

"My generation, the notion of marketing your own copy, that was like dirty," he told the Nieman Journalism Lab last year. "You know, don't make me get near that. That's somebody else's job. But in fact, now, marketing—we don't call it that, but that's a big part of what online journalists do. Figuring out which blogs they need to be in touch with in order to keep their audience together, using Twitter to drive traffic to your stuff, figuring out the right mix."

It's not just marketing, for Murray. It's figuring out what you are going to write and knowing how it may be received: "I mean, the art of a good blog is figuring out the right mix between the piece that you know is going to get maximum search-engine hits to the piece that really defines what you're doing that's uniquely valuable. . . . So all of that, which is part of the job of building a community, building an audience—those are totally new skills." If you "friend" Alan on Facebook, you'll see a steady stream of recommendations of articles—mostly but not always from the *Journal*—that he thinks are worth reading.

Murray is the vanguard in such thinking, but more of his colleagues are coming around to the same notions.

Most of the people we've met so far—Michelle Nicolosi, Jon Lansner, Larry Schwartz, Scott Lewis, and Angela O'Connor, for instance—fully embrace such tools and have made them a part of their routines. They use the social tools to research, to connect with audiences, and to promote.

Some news companies are ahead of the pack. By the middle of last year, *The New York Times* had more than a quarter of a million Twitter followers and had smartly established separate Twitter channels for areas like books and arts, knowing that niching of social media makes it work better.

On many newspaper or broadcast sites, we see Twitter and Facebook icons popping up, offering new ways to connect journalists and readers. Still, media does find itself largely behind its audience—

this is this repeated story in the digital revolution—and the amount of added traffic or revenue bang for the social buck is so far hard to measure.

Why does Old Media lag here?

David Scott is well positioned to give us a tour of this landscape. He's a former Big Media guy, having worked in business development for Knight Ridder Information. David can tell you great stories about selling U.S. news content in Asia and about the difficulty American companies had in adjusting to international marketing.

Now, though, he's much in demand for applying his expertise to this point of how marketing has been revolutionized by the Web.

So why might Old Media be slow to the dance?

Scott has one notion: "Social media technologies do not make a brand viral; they merely allow consumers to tell others about good brands." In fact, Old Media has tended to put the usual stuff on the Web, make it Facebook-able or able to be Twitter-ized, but it hasn't used the new tools in new ways very much.

Scott's latest book, *World Wide Rave* (Wiley, 2009), tells his readers how to use the Web "to get millions of people to spread your ideas and share your stories." He's basically telling people that using the Old Media-mediated methods are over. Relatively speaking, they are expensive, time-consuming, and inefficient.

He notes such phenomena as IBM's *Art of the Sale* videos, *The Wizarding World of Harry Potter,* at Universal Orlando, and the *Girls Fight Back* self-defense videos. Few of the "raves"—these popular phenomena—touch on anything news companies produce.

For instance, Scott proposes e-books as great sales starters, basically offering for free some niche content so that readers will be enticed to buy more. E-books, or e-magazines, could be great tantalizers for news companies eager to sell niche products—in health or travel, for instance—for a fee, but I've not yet seen that done well.

Or think about data. People love data, and lists. The Real Clear Politics poll box was a must stop for many during the 2008 election season, and RCP smartly distributed the box around the Web with links back to its own site. Publishers need more hooks to start some raves of their own.

As with blogging, social marketing is just another tool to be added to the increasingly crowded skills tool chest, as we'll explore in the next chapter.

While social media is all the buzz, there's nothing like that old standby, TV, to drive traffic. Robert Allbritton, scion of a media family, knew that. So when he and two news executives from old-line media established Politico three years ago, media cross-promotion was in the original game plan. In fact, CEO Allbritton and editors Jim VandeHei and John Harris play their news directly to the "news cycle." They time and pitch their journalism—having engendered some within-the-fraternity derision for that—knowing what TV, the blogosphere, and the wires need and precisely when they need it.

In "Itch the Niche," I noted how Politico had made political news sexy, made it a sport, and has profited well. Its correspondents pop up all over cable. Always in the background: the Politico logo, well designed and well communicated over TV. Visit the Politico office in the shadow of Capitol Hill, and you see the same brand banner that has quickly seeped into national political consciousness.

Not only does Politico match its journalism timing to its understanding of media, it works the media. Even when it had only a hundred staffers, three of them focused on media. They make and maintain relationships with bookers, know what the networks are looking for, and pitch, pitch, pitch.

Most media companies, of course, promote their own Web sites using their own products and have long assumed that yelling through their own megaphones would suffice. Politico, on the other hand, understood that its Web site in and of itself was no known quantity. It needed to build its brand through others' brands and placement, and it set out—brilliantly and successfully—to do just that. Now its Web site is among the Top 20 in the country, ahead of *The Miami Herald*, the *San Jose Mercury News*, and the Minneapolis *Star Tribune*. Getting covered demands a mix of the right story, the right brand, and the right personality. Politico's got a number of reporters who excel at the art.

Look at one of Politico's fellow political start-ups, and you can see the direct role of a big personality. Like William Randolph Hearst (and Oprah), Arianna Huffington put her name right on the company and the product. Her personality served as a magnet both for readers and blogging contributors—who receive no payment—and the enterprise built from there into, like Politico, a Top 20 news site.

It's a lesson that new players—from Politico to Huffington Post to GlobalPost to *Slate* and *Salon*—force themselves to learn just to get noticed in a busy world. Older players like *The New York Times* and *The Wall Street Journal* are learning it more slowly, but now increasingly turn up on NPR and the cable news shows.

Add up the great splintering of media, the breakup of long-held monopolies, and the low-barrier entry points enjoyed by so many emerging start-ups, and we find that the new key for new media is being found and shared. That's why mastering the old—TV, TV, TV—and the new social tools are a must-learn for news media.

So in this great splintering, let's consider it from a *marketer's* point of view: How do I find the right person at the right media to talk about my company?

The room at the San Francisco Marriott was full, packed with a couple of hundred people for the In-Bound Marketing summit. I'd been invited to participate in a panel entitled "Media in Transition: The Future of News in a Democratized World." I'd done many of those, but mostly for audiences closer to the news business themselves.

This was an audience of marketers trying to get a better understanding of and an edge in the viral marketing that the Web has set afire. If the media are trying to figure out how to harness viral marketing, marketers are trying to figure out how to harness the new, diverse, and diffused media. This, then, was a gathering that represented the flip side.

As we panelists spoke, the audience was Tweeting away. Some picked up and relayed to their Twitter followers what we said in 140 characters or fewer—"I don't think anyone's gonna figure out a new biz model. Huge newsrooms were a historical accident," for example. Others picked out numbers and flung the factoids into the Twittersphere. A few offered instant critiques of a panelist's grip on reality. All the Tweets were neatly organized under the hash mark of #IMS09, with the conference Tweet production highly ranked—everything is ranked—on Twitter that day.

For the conference and for the panelists, you couldn't ask for a better publicity machine. And it didn't cost a dime. All "user-generated," quite enthusiastically.

The summit offers a good snapshot of the emerging marketer's art. The new viral communication—Twitter, Facebook, and to some degree LinkedIn—can be quite powerful. Yet all these messages are tossed out into a seemingly bottomless digital ocean, flowing by all who are participating minute by minute.

While these marketers were participating in this social revolution, they had come to the conference to get tips on how best to harness the power for their companies, services and products. And, coming full circle, they wanted to get an answer to one prominent question: How do we now approach the media, as they splinter and split?

It's a tough question.

I can see it from both sides. I was in a newsroom for many years, on the receiving end of story pitches. Now as an analyst, consultant, author, and blogger—many of us have many hats these days—I can see it from the other end, figuring out how my work gets the play I want it to.

So here are my suggestions for marketers in this new world:

- DIY: Many marketers are used to working in larger organizations with *other* people in charge of reaching out, watching metrics, or crafting a message. The new world requires less of waiting for someone else to jump into the fray—old world and new, they often don't—and more of doing it yourself. Direct one-to-one and one-to-many communication are hallmarks of all these new technologies. Use them yourself, making direct connections—people are surprisingly open and respond—and learn.
- Find the networks you need: Whether it's the right hash mark on Twitter or relevant Facebook group, the odds are that the influencers you want to reach are already organized and are willing to receive useful pitches. Lose yourself in these social networks for a day, and you'll be amazed at who you can connect with, for free.
- Beyond linking up, become a social creature. In Silicon Valley we call it eating your own dog food. That means actually using—day in and day out—the products you need to understand. As a news

industry analyst covering the transition from print to digital, blogging not only gave me a platform; it taught me how blogging would change journalism itself.

- Get free customer feedback. Learn from Google—it's all beta, baby. Your words, your message, your pitch, your service can all be "experimental," subject to tweaking. Use the Web—and your new friends—to test the pitches and refine them. In the old world, you had to employ expensive and often unreliable focus groups, which gave a finite sense of how your product might do in the marketplace. Now you can keep testing, keep tweaking, keep asking.
- Use new ways to measure your success. For this, I'll borrow directly from David Scott's *World Wide Rave*. Here are his six ways to measure success in this world:

1. How many people are exposed to your ideas?
2. How many people are downloading your stuff?
3. How often are bloggers writing about you and your ideas?
4. (And what are those bloggers saying?)
5. Where are you appearing in search results for important phrases?
6. How many people are engaging with you and are making the choice to speak to you about your offerings?

That list is a long way from just counting sales leads.

My sense is that just as in news wrangling, the aggregation of news, we'll see smart aggregators moving into this new media marketing wilderness.

A few are, already. Take the story of Peter Shankman. He has described himself as a guy who loves cats, skydiving, and running marathons. He also has traditional PR roots, his Geek Factory business having worked with American Express and Disney, among many others.

Now, he runs the philanthropically named Help a Reporter Out. It's not a charity, though. Shankman is a new middleman. On the one hand, he has built up a list of 25,000 reporters who need sources. On the other, he has 75,000 marketers looking for publicity.

Shankman's digital genius is in using the Web to connect up the source seekers with those who legitimately think themselves to be useful sources. If it's really urgent, Shankman uses the most with-it connector, Twitter.

His initial revenue source: advertising, which runs on all those e-mails linking the two groups. My guess: He ends up making more bucks around the data he's collecting, niching the marketers, niching the reporters, and counting the top story topics named.

Viral marketing is just one of the many news skills we see in increasingly demand, as new journalists enter the field and midcareer ones try to figure out which end is up. We're ready to look at the new skill sets in the next chapter.

11

For Journalists' Jobs, It's Back to the Future

If Moses had been paid newspaper rates for the Ten Commandments, he might have written the Two Thousand Commandments.—ISAAC BASHEVIS SINGER

The fact that a man is a newspaper reporter is evidence of some flaw of character.—LYNDON B. JOHNSON

Allen Hall, built in 1954, is ready for the news and advertising revolutions.

Long the home of the University of Oregon School of Journalism in Eugene, it hosts one of the larger media studies programs in the nation. Courses on news, magazines, advertising, broadcast, and public relations all have long and storied traditions; many of its professors live on in their students' memories. In 2002, the school updated itself physically.

New digital newsrooms replaced the old, and the modern technological tools of the trade are in place. It's the school's curriculum that's undergoing the most change, though, as Dean Tim Gleason and the faculty try to make their coursework relevant to the roiling trade.

They've done a lot, but still Gleason worries: "In the past, parents used to say, 'I'm so glad he's a journalism major rather than an English major.' That may change."

That, of course, is the crux of an issue in journalism education: Exactly what kind of world might these students be entering? Will there in fact be jobs for them?

Jobs are one issue—for new graduates and veteran journalists alike. "Skills" shape the other big question. If in fact, livelihoods can be nurtured in this new digital age, exactly what kinds of skills are needed?

That brings us to Law No. 11: For Journalists' Jobs, It's Back to the Future.

CONSIDER:

- Despite the well-publicized layoffs in traditional media outlets, journalism schools are still packed with students. Applications— perhaps a bit recession-fueled—have been up in double digits from Columbia and Stanford to the University of Colorado (up 11 percent) and the University of Maryland (up 25 percent). In 2007, U.S. journalism and mass communications schools hosted nearly 200,000 undergraduates, up from 130,000 in 1995.
- A big generational divide is disconnecting yesterday's journalists from tomorrow's as the adoption of new tools and techniques shows itself to be uneven.
- Middle-class salaries are giving way to a freelance economy, and that carries all kinds of challenges for those getting into the business.

We see how there is a certain retro quality to the landscape unfolding. It wasn't until after World War II, as daily newspapers thinned out and monopolies were born, that we saw the creation of huge newsrooms. It wasn't until then that daily journalism became a desirable career, paying good middle-class wages and offering near-lifetime job guarantees.

Revisit journalism in the early part of the twentieth century, the *Front Page* era, and you'd see the hardscrabble side of the daily trade. Reporters were far more itinerate, right up there with actors; you might not have wanted your daughter to marry one. Pay rates were more Dickensian—per word, per piece—than salaried. A forty-hour Monday through Friday workweek was unheard of. Reporters, less high-sounding than journalists, pieced together a living, balancing multiple assignments, often from several publications. (See "Newsonomics 101: The Seven Dirty Words You Can No Longer Say in Newspaper Buildings" page 190.)

That's the world to which we seem to be returning. Well, maybe not the part about whiskey flasks falling out of the coat pockets, but the piecing-it-together part.

Take the many Pro-Am contributors of the companies in this book. Many contributing writers for GlobalPost, New West, Politico, MinnPost, Voice of San Diego, and Marketplace, and numerous others all take less than a full-time wage. It can range from a hundred bucks a month to a stipend of a thousand. Or they can be paid by the article. Or in the case of Huffington Post, their sole compensation will be in getting their name out there, legitimized, so that somebody else will pay them something for their writing, speaking, or consulting work.

It's a Gig Economy, a kind of new freelancer's life, and it makes those who have had the good civil service–like middle-class jobs highly uncomfortable.

If you're twenty-two and entering the market, it's a challenge. If you're fifty-two and just got one of those thousands of pink slips, some months of severance, and a good-bye, it can be terrifying. I can't count the number of journalists who've told me that they can't believe this irony: After covering so many trades that ended badly and in massive job losses—fill in "autoworkers," "steelworkers," "forest product workers," "fisherman"—they find themselves subjected to the same injury. The job they had planned to do until they retired no longer exists.

The sad truth is that many of these jobs will never come back. As we've seen, the new Newsonomics simply doesn't support the number of jobs and the wage scales previous generations enjoyed. That doesn't mean that journalism won't get done, or even that we as readers will suffer eternally because of the dramatic change to the industry. That does mean that the skills contemporary journalists— whoever they work for—will need are changing dramatically. We can look at those skills in a couple of ways, the journalistic tools of the trade now required and the business smarts more independent workers need to survive and prosper.

You hear the mantra over and over again.

The Wall Street Journal's Alan Murray: "Find people who can write several times a day, get juiced about it, and find other people who want to do it. It's up to managers to get the right people in the right jobs."

Right people. Right jobs. Right skills. Those are the people who will keep their jobs in cutbacks, and those who will get hired.

What are those skills?

We might think of them as tweener skills. I first heard the term "tweener" when I arrived in San Jose to work at Knight Ridder New Media in 1997. Then it described the kind of part-editorial, part-techie mind-set and skill set that was highly useful in the Web's earlier days. Content people had to do a fair amount formatting, coding, and work-arounds to get what they wanted on the digital page.

Now, tweener speaks to the kind of in-between transitional skills we all need. We wear lots of different hats, as journalism producers, software users, communications testers, and marketers. The multitasking Barack Obama is our modern role model. His pronouncement "The President needs to do more than one thing at a time" contrasted his work approach with that of John McCain's, and I think it's symbolic of the era. If the president can multitask, journalists need to be able to move among thinking, writing, and communication quickly as well.

In fact, tweener skills now cross daily between the work of journalism and the work of the business of journalism. A print-turned-online editor told me that his new job description included figuring out how to get the company's content distributed and syndicated on the Web, and that meant interviewing vendors, doing business reference checks, and contracting—all skills relatively new to him at age fifty-four. He's not alone. We're seeing groups like Knight Digital Media Center offering News Entrepreneur Boot Camps to teach a variety of these tweener skills.

Certainly, the first that comes to mind is the newest—the set of social networking skills. Twitter, Facebook, and LinkedIn have become, overnight, great new tools that allow journalists to find sources, connect with audiences, and get tips. In a sense, they are no-brainers. Longtime daily journalist Gina Chen offers a lot of good advice about using the new tools—how journalists can get started on Twitter and why journalists should blog—on her Web site, Savethe-Media. (See "Q & A: Gina Chen," page 195.)

New West's Jonathan Weber had recently started using Twitter when I talked to him last spring. He found it a surprisingly effective new tool of journalism in covering a trial: "You do the same things you always do. You go to the trial. You talk to the lawyers. You figure out what the hell is going on. I was Twittering the trial, and I'd not done that before. It's more the commentary [that the readers like] than the news. A friend of mine said, 'You're like the person in the room who really knows what's going on and whispers it to someone.'"

Which sums it up well. The news imparts more than facts; there's knowledge and perspective. Again, as we've seen in the role of blogging, social networking is just another cool set of tools. It changes the how of journalism, but not its core.

It's also about getting handy with a camcorder and digital audio.

We've seen and heard legions of emerging journalists grabbing multimedia in recent years. One sticks in my memory, particularly.

As Sarah Palin became the surprise Republican vice presidential candidate in spring 2008, I recall finding the work of Kyle Hopkins on the *Anchorage Daily News* site. Hopkins, a political reporter, had shot lots of press conference footage, coverage that became all the more interesting as allegations of the governor's political interference in state police business surfaced. He was one print reporter wielding a sometimes unsteady camcorder. It was journalism, though, and it made a difference. Sometimes we just need journalists to be there, with the right tools of the trade.

Among all these new, flexible, multimedia, forward-reaching skills, the bedrock journalistic skills must form the foundation.

Reporting. Interviewing. Editing. Writing. These basic tools remain important, even though the way they're done—think e-mail interviews, access to deep, instant archives for research, and writing shorter, succinctly, for the Web—is morphing.

These foundational values, though, still need to be in place at the journalism schools, even as the faculties restructure the whole curricula.

In a nutshell, the educators—as well as the best newsroom editors managing change—will tell you there is one constant: It is still about storytelling. And, oh, the stories that audio, video, Flash, reader interaction, and other technologies can help you tell better.

Right in that bedrock are the long-established values of journalism—the "without fear or favor" proclaimed by *The New York Times*'s Adolph Ochs long ago—and the integrity of the trade.

In a multimedia, anyone-can-be-a-publisher age offering the potential of great abuse of trust and fact, what journalists cannot do is forget where they came from or why they do the work they do.

One place those skills are being developed is in the journalism schools.

At Oregon, it's about "integrating skills sets," starting with a new two-term hands-on gateway curriculum. At Northwestern, the new master's journalism program curriculum starts with the same "content-audience-business" model, but acknowledges that much is now up in the air. "We don't know how to do it. The industry doesn't know how to it," says Rich Gordon, a professor and director of digital innovation, a good thinker on this evolution, who is just acknowledging how much is uncharted territory. Just as the news industry is being reinvented, so are Northwestern's programs and emphases.

Oregon's dean Tim Gleason is concerned about how fast times are changing. "How long do you expect students who don't use the [traditional] media to walk in the door? . . . We are threatened by irrelevance."

As Nicholas Lemann, dean of the Columbia School of Journalism, has pointed out, people have rarely decided to go into the trade to cash in. "I've never met a single person in thirty-five years who went into journalism out of pure economic reason." Still, it may become harder to justify studying for a graduate journalism degree, which can require an investment of $50,000 or more from the better schools. After all, how many years of low-wage employment will it take to pay that sum off?

To the cost question, Gordon says he makes the point to students and parents that journalism skills are useful—and transferable—to many fields outside the news business.

There's little doubt we're seeing the opening of a big generational divide in journalism. Adoption of and comfort with new journalism tools largely varies with age, though there are many exceptions. It's that divide—the news industry's own digital divide—that poses a major challenge for midcareer journalists.

For these Gen-X and baby-boom journalists—or at least the 80 percent or so who still have the jobs they had five years ago—it is gut-check time. Do they have the will to make big changes in how they do things?

In a 2009 column, Maureen Dowd's anti-Twitter rant stands as one indicator: "I would rather be tied up to stakes in the Kalahari Desert, have honey poured over me and red ants eat out my eyes than open a Twitter account."

Newsroom culture is a powerful thing. Over the decades, we've seen great craft attitudes: integrity, accuracy, making the daily miracle deadline whatever it took. We've also seen self-destructive craft attitudes: a sense of entitlement, of not-invented-here, of passive-aggressiveness. The latter set of attitudes has greatly retarded the successful transition from mainly print or broadcast newsrooms to hybrid ones. Those attitudes, combined with management's strategic miscues, have left things in the state they are in.

So how do we change culture? Old Media has been trying for more than a decade, with quite mixed results. There's little doubt that bankruptcies, massive job cuts, and operating losses have stunned workforces. As the stun wears off, culture change can happen from within—a real embracing of new methods and technologies by the existing staff—or from without. The without solution—more rapid replacement of experienced midcareer people with more flexible, multiskilled youngsters—is already well underway.

This generational change is transforming journalism. It is bringing fresh perspective and freer storytelling. It also leaves behind vast storehouses of institutional memory. When many twenty-five-year-plus journalists disappear from their desks, seemingly overnight, they take with them the knowledge of where lots of bodies are buried in their communities. In stable times, newsrooms worked under virtual apprenticeship models, with younger journalists absorbing the knowledge (and bad craft habits) of the vets. Now that system is being swept away.

Given the Newsonomics landscape, there's some inevitability to that loss. Still, I'd like to see innovative ways to connect up this spirited new generation with the experience and community knowledge of those who have left.

The learning, of course, goes two ways. We're in an age where the young teach their elders lots about adapting to the new world.

For all of us, it's learn and teach, teach and learn. As Tim Gleason says of the program's new mandates: "We want to create space so they [the students] teach us and each other."

Another issue of skills and culture: math. It was one of those small moments that speak volumes. I'd finished a day of consulting at the *San Antonio Express-News*. I'd done my presentation on the trend lines of the business, taken questions, and gotten the usual reaction: engagement, worry, and some mix of defeatism and hopefulness.

After the presentation, one of the newspaper's section editors came up, thanked me, and said, "That was very interesting. Looking at all those numbers, I hadn't understood how deep the problem is. I don't do math."

NEWSONOMICS 101: The Seven Dirty Words You Can No Longer Say in Newspaper Buildings

Where is George Carlin when we need him?

The news business is about words. Anyone who has been in a newsroom will tell you that hardly any word is taboo. In fact, when my friend Deborah Howell left the *Saint Paul Pioneer Press* newsroom as top editor in 1990, the newsroom offered a spirited good-bye—and made side bets on how many times Deborah would use her favorite expletive in her farewell speech.

(continued)

Times, though, now are tough. So, just what might be the Seven Dirty Words You Can't Say in Newspaper Buildings today?

Newspaper: The word itself speaks of an almost bygone era.

News: "News" itself is problematic. Companies don't want to produce general news. They want news they can sell advertising around, and that means niches—business readers, techies, health enthusiasts, action movie watchers, not perusers of general news.

Paper: That one's now worse than "news." With newspaper companies using a little less than half of what they used five years ago, paper's out. Pixels are in.

Circulation: With the old-age disease of arteriosclerosis ("degenerative changes in the arteries, characterized by thickening of the vessel walls and accumulation of calcium with consequent loss of elasticity and lessened blood flow") setting in with ferocity (three percentage-point declines each six-month reporting period for five years now), publishers will tell you to remember to add together print readers and online readers. It's not circulation. It's *readership*.

Staff: Reporters have always been a necessary pain in the butt, but now they're, well, less necessary. With less newsprint to fill, fewer dollars left to pay people, who wants "staff"?

Editor: You remember, the *guy* who decided the news we'd see the next morning, the gatekeeper we discussed in Law No. 1? In May last year, the *East Oregonian* newspaper in Pendleton, Oregon, laid off its top editor, saying it could no longer afford the position. Editors cost a lot of money, more than reporters. Can't algorithms just replace them?

Default: Consider this a double entendre. Default as in, we're not going to make that debt payment (the numerous bankruptcies and near bankruptcies we're seeing in the newspaper industry). And, as in, (de) fault is not mine. Google's Eric Schmidt and craigslist's Craig Newmark have both said, hey, don't blame *us* for changing the news and classified games.

"I don't do math." Now one editor not doing math isn't a big problem. Her statement, though, revived memories of my ten-year stint at the *Saint Paul Pioneer Press*, from the mideighties to the midnineties. Finding good business reporters on staff was tough; in fact, we often heard variants on "I don't do math."

For all those who think of themselves as word people, not math people, the world is a tougher place. It didn't just take the financial meltdown to tell us numbers—and their analysis—do matter. How can you really cover city hall or planning or even the local sports franchises these days if you don't, in the words of another era, follow the money (or "do the math"). Financial illiteracy almost seemed like a badge of honor in those bygone journalism days. Now it's a prescription for career limitations and job elimination.

For journalists themselves, having at their fingertips deep, deep databases (which once were the province solely of "investigative" reporters), knowing how to read an annual budget or a 10-K disclosure is essential. Northwestern's Journalism School is "upping the ante," says Rich Gordon. "We want students to be literate in business and the use of data in their work." If that's a skill they need to advance their own journalism, it's also now a skill they need to advance themselves.

In the gig economy, journalists are in charge of their own careers, their own finances, their own pensions, their own health care; they can't look to companies to do that planning for them. For midcareer journalists, it's going to be about self-teaching, deep immersion in everything from the daily *Wall Street Journal* to the *Dummies* series to local classes.

It's not just in newsroomlike skills that the news industry is behind the times. News has always been a business, but its longtime stability has made it insular. Contributing to their own demise, newspaper and broadcast companies have found themselves possessing too few of the skills the new Web *business* demanded. Here are just four:

Marketing. Good luck trying to find a line for marketing expense in a newspaper company budget. No wonder broadcasters and publishers have done such a poor job of marketing their emerging digital selves. They did so little, save for in-house promotion, in the old world.

Business Development. Huh? You mean selling ads. The whole idea of finding new ways to work with companies that could be helpful partners—distributing your products, giving you story links, putting your reporters on air—has been alien. The skill set hardly existed. As the frenzy of deal making happened all around them, early newspaper company executives were the targets of jokes about their cluelessness in knowing how to work the new landscape. Later, as a cadre of managers did learn such skills, they've often found themselves deeply frustrated with their own companies' abilities to move decisively and quickly. Many have now left Old Media.

Audience Development. You mean circulation? Winning on the Web means crunching lots of data, applying the deep lessons of comparative search-engine optimization, search-engine marketing, ad sales revenue optimization, and conversion ratios. It's a skill start-ups know they need—and are willing to pay for. It's a skill few Old Media companies have sufficiently invested in.

Consultative Sales. Old Media sales staffs have been derisively called order takers. While not universally true, it has been too true. Modern sales requires listening to merchants' market needs and tailoring new ad programs to them. The Yahoo Newspaper Consortium has spurred a minirevolution here, but there's a ways to go.

Long story short. The new Newsonomics requires a new group of savvy business operators who can help revive the trade.

Media, of course, may well want to make it seem that their staff is big and full-time, even if it's not. Listen to the Marketplace program, and you'll hear "expert commentators on the day's news." They all sound authoritative, journalistically credible—and full-time. But they're not all full-time.

It's a great example of journalism that is rolling with the times. The newer operations use correspondents, who are often stringers, to use the old-fashioned terms for journalists working by the piece. Stringer, or stipend-based, journalism lets pinched-for-cash news operations do more with less. For the stringers, it's more often now a matter of stringing together assignments from a number of workplaces and balancing them.

It's the gig economy under way, and that's where many journalists like prolific tech writer Glenn Fleishman lives. (See "Q & A: Glenn Fleishman," page 196.)

His experience is not a new one for many magazine journalists. That has long been a freelance trade. Now even as magazine journalism and its assignments tighten up, newspaper journalists are seeing their work lives come to resemble those of their magazine colleagues.

We can see this gig economy also in the start-ups we've discussed: GlobalPost, MinnPost, and NewWest—some of our best incubators of impressive digital reporting—pay most of their contributors in the thousands and hundreds. They provide a stipend and hope their journalists can piece together a living through other work, until the publications can achieve a scale that will allow them to employ full-time reporters.

For pros like Dave Beal, it has been a curious transition. Beal had been a well-read business columnist at the *Saint Paul Pioneer Press*, where he worked for a dozen years. Now he's writing for MinnPost weekly, one of ten staffers paid a monthly retainer of $600 or so. He writes at least weekly, with greater payments for more work. Another forty journalists contribute on a similar basis.

What Beal says is typical of other vets' reaction to his invitation to participate: "[Joel] Kramer's thing is uphill, like so many of these other pilot projects. But he has gotten so many good people involved that it's just impossible to not take up the invitation to be a part of it. The mission, to go in and get real news that's not being covered much anymore, is absolutely spot on. So even though bringing this off will be very difficult, an unusually large number of planets have come into alignment for MinnPost." It's that alignment that offers journalists hope in a grim time.

Maybe, just maybe, there is an upward trajectory to be found out of the pain.

We can anticipate the greatest number of new jobs in journalism will be in this gig economy. If you can believe the forecasting of the Bureau of Labor Statistics, by 2016 the number of positions for entry-level reporters and news anchors will increase 2 percent, while those for experienced writers and editors will grow 10 percent. That's quite a small increase over that period of time. It points to a reshuffling of the deck, but not a lot of growth. Then, again, take it from an analyst: Any 2016 prediction is like gypsy fortune-telling.

In this emerging freelance economy, journalists must distinguish and differentiate themselves from, ironically, the growing amateur masses. Many thousands of people are subject experts or passionate about some topic—and willing to write about it for next to nothing. Some of the companies I've noted, like Helium, have partnered with major media companies like Hearst, and are making it easier for all these to get published. For Hearst, it is increasingly able to "buy" cheaper content through the Heliums, and that poses a problem for professional freelancers. Can they both price themselves high enough to make a living and low enough to get jobs?

We began this book talking about the great transformation of news in our time, and we've come back here to its basics—reporting. There's a growing gap between the reporting we're getting and what we need. Let's conclude our Newsonomics tour by seeing what it will take to mind that gap, and others, too.

Q & A: Gina Chen

GINA CHEN *is a prolific, highly socially oriented journalist. Her SavetheMedia.com blog is a treasure trove of tips, especially around social media. After spending twenty years as a reporter and editor for* The Post-Standard *in Syracuse, New York, she is now pursuing a doctorate in communications at the S. I. Newhouse School of Public Communications at Syracuse University.*

Q: What's the most interesting unintended consequence that you've derived from your Twitter experience?

A: I expected Twitter would be useful for promoting my blogs, getting a handle on what topics are buzzing, and finding new blogs to read. But I never imagined its immediate power to get questions answered—from how to get gum out of my daughter's sweater to how to define journalism.

Q: What have you learned from watching how young journalists use social media?

A: I've taught a few college classes on how journalists can use Facebook and Twitter. I find some young people are eager to translate their expansive personal understanding of social media to the professional realm. But some, surprisingly, are entrenched in doing things the old way. I think that sometimes it's hard for younger people to see social media as a journalistic tool because it's so intrinsic to their personal lives. For old-timers like me, social media weren't part of my life until I applied it to journalism, so it seems a natural fit.

Q: What do you tell young journalists about the trade they are now getting into?

A: I tell young journalists it's an exciting time to be entering the business because everything is in flux. Our whole notion of what constitutes journalism is being redefined. They can be part of creating this new world, and that's exciting. But it's a challenging time. They won't have the luxury to learn on the job as I did. They'll need to start out with stellar reporting, writing, and interviewing skills along with a broad knowledge of using multimedia tools, social media, and marketing ideas to reach an audience. They'll need an entrepreneurial spirit and understand how to promote themselves as a brand.

Q: What lesson in digital media do you wish you'd learned faster?

A: When I started blogging two years ago, I knew almost nothing about it. I wish I'd known then the power of linking to other sites and becoming part of the existing community of bloggers in a niche. Tapping into a community works much better than trying to create your own. I also wish I'd understood the basics of search-engine optimization sooner, so I could have started earlier to get my blog indexed in Google and drive more traffic to it.

Q & A: Glenn Fleishman

I first met Glenn Fleishman when his dad, Charlie, sold advertising for my alternative weekly, the Willamette Valley Observer. *Reconnecting with Glenn years later, he told me that his early exposure to journalism, as a teenager visiting our late-seventies newsroom, had set him on his career course.*

His work as a technology journalist is found all over the Web, and he has done seven blogs. I asked him about the freelance life these days.

Q: How many hats are you currently wearing, different relationships with publishers, your own work sites, etc.?

A: Several.

- Traditional freelancer. I pitch various publications on a regular basis, with the top-line ones being *The Economist*, *The Seattle Times*, *Popular Science*, and *Macworld*. I usually wind up getting bites to write one to three *Economist* articles a year, two to four *PopSci* pieces, six to eight *Seattle Times* articles, and a dozen or more *MacWorld* articles.
- Traditional feature stringer. Publications call me to write for them, mostly from the above, but also, when some Web sites and one-off print relationships where they have a topic, need a writer, I oblige. I usually have more leverage in fees in those cases, of course.
- Columnist, *Seattle Times*. I write a column every four weeks about the Mac.
- My own Wi-Fi blog. I started Wi-Fi Networking News in 2001, and I had a fellow freelancer working part-time during the heyday a few years ago, but it's mostly been me for the last eight years as editor-reporter. The site at one point got about 300K page views a month; it's down to 60K page views partly because the industry matured to ship products that work and aren't confusing to use. Good for my readers, bad for readership! The blog has morphed a bit into an industry news site from a more general how-to–breaking news–reportage site.
- Contributing editor and programmer for TidBITS, a Mac journal. TidBITS (www.tidbits.com) is by our research the longest-running continuously published e-mail newsletter on the Internet, having started up in 1990. The Web site came much later, of course, and we now have about 30K e-mail subscribers and 250K monthly page impressions, and more of a publish-to-Web approach than we used to when the e-mail newsletter predominated. I've hand-built the content management system we use, and I write regularly and am involved in structural and business decisions.

Q: Do you feel like you are part of the new(er) gig economy in journalism, as independent contracting becomes more dominant than single-employer "jobs"?

A: Yes and no. I've either worked for companies I started or for myself since 1995 (with a notable six-month stint at Amazon being an exception), and started freelancing in 1994 for trade magazines. So many of my relationships date back before any real sea change happened in journalism.

I haven't seen much of a change in how I work over the last decade, just an ever-changing mix of publications. In the early double-oughts, I was writing for *Wired, Business 2.0* (as an every-four-weeks columnist being paid a retainer, of all things), eCompany Now, *Fortune*, and *The New York Times. Business 2.0* shifted focus, and all the editors I knew left. ECompany Now was sort of merged into *B2.0*. *Wired* editors left and changed, and I stopped getting pitches answered, which is impolite. The editor I knew at *Fortune* had his freelance budget slashed. And so on.

12

Mind the Gaps

I understand that you want to make finance entertaining, but it's not a game. I can't tell you how angry that makes me. That tells me you all know what the banks were doing and yet were touting it for months and months. . . . To pretend that this was some crazy once-in-a-lifetime tsunami that no one saw coming is disingenuous at best and criminal at worst.—**JON STEWART (to CNBC's Jim Cramer)**

We can't solve problems by using the same kind of thinking we used when we created them.—**ALBERT EINSTEIN**

It was a bubble moment. In 1999, a couple of years after jumping headfirst into the new digital business of Knight Ridder, I found myself at Excite headquarters in Redwood City. Excite was a great bubble company, made euphoric by its intoxicating growth and heedless about its small revenues. Walk into the Excite building, and you'd think you were in a funhouse, bicycles suspended from ceilings, large slides for employees to frolic down. Colorfully painted walls, colorfully named conference rooms. The whole package.

You've heard this Silicon Valley story, or one like it: Six Stanford undergrads meet in a freshman dorm and decide to strike out on their own after graduation, for the fun of it, "unencumbered by reality." They start a "company" over burritos at Rosita's Taqueria and before you know it, they are rich enough to tear down monster houses in order to build monster compounds.

I had my meeting with the Excite "folks," and I had a half hour to return e-mails, before heading back to the office. Excite had thoughtfully designated several visitor offices off its lobby, complete with Internet access. I picked one, but got little work done. The show through the office window was just too entertaining.

Every few minutes, a new small group of visitors would arrive. Inevitably, they'd be dressed in standard business wear, suits and ties, and carrying briefcases tough enough to repel a bullet. The receptionist would greet them and sign them in. Then, out of the blissful chaos of the Internet start-up, you'd see one or two Excite executives come out, shake hands, and take the visitors to an interior conference room.

For the Excite execs, it wasn't suits and ties. It was jeans, denims, and polo shirts, maybe a pack slung over the arm. It was work as leisure.

My little voyeuristic adventure ended, but the impression has long stayed with me: You could see the changing of the guard in that Excite lobby. You could see the guys with the emerging power—the guys and gals with the distribution pipes—and you could see those with the waning power.

On the waning end were my company, Knight Ridder, then the second-biggest newspaper publisher in the country, and really all of Old Media. Those with less power had to dress up (or thought they had to) because they were the sellers; those with more power, the buyers, wore—and did—what they pleased. The choice of clothes said volumes about how the power equation was changing.

The Excite experience exposed a change in the landscape and a gap. That was a gap between who had the power and who was grabbing the power.

The more I've thought about the emerging Newsonomics of the trade, the more I see it in terms of gaps. And as the helpful Brits remind us on the Tube, the gaps must be minded.

Today, the gaps may seem more like one endless crevasse. You know, the kind of scene you see in one of those Imax mountain-climbing movies. You see infinite ice below and say, "How the hell are they going to get over that?"

It is quite a crevasse. Too little revenue. Incomplete skills. Big cultural issues.

On the other side of that gap, we can see bright blue sky. We can see that our ability to produce great reporting, to produce storytelling that pleases most of our senses, and to dig deeper into data and secrets that powerful interests don't want us to know. We can also see that our ability to tell stories, and to get them out more quickly and more widely than ever before possible, has never been greater.

We can see the blue sky up ahead, but we can't, today, quite figure out how to get to it.

So as we close our view of one world that has fallen apart and the building blocks being used to erect a new world, let's take a quick view of these gaps and what can be done about them.

The Money Gap. Let's start with the one on everyone's mind. The tens of billions of dollars that sustained news businesses, allowing them to pay tens of thousands of journalists won't be coming back. The new building blocks of the digital ad revolution will support heavier and heavier loads. They'll pay, slowly and over time, for more news to be reported and written by professionals. While they'll never pay the freight that the print business used to, by 2015, they'll pay for more then they do today. What about the *rest* of what's needed?

The question we face is how we're going to pay professionals to get us the news we need. As we've seen, new funding techniques are being tested. We see NPR-like membership models, community and national foundation interest, civic-minded investors, and event-oriented business models. We hear about nonprofits and community trusts. Within the Digital Dozen, we see news businesses absorbed, leveraged, and (maybe) protected by global conglomerates. We talk about new tax approaches that may fund news and information, as our Western European neighbors have been doing for decades. We see experiments with micropayments and new online subscription initiatives. Finally, we see the potential of a reckoning with the big search-engine aggregators who, today, get a pretty big piece of the pie and have problems with sharing.

I'm fairly agnostic about which of these many ideas will take root. What I am sure about is that it's a big solution we need. It may well embrace a number of those ideas, but it needs to be big, hundreds of millions big, and we won't get there incrementally with nickels, dimes, and tin cups.

We're a robust democracy, and we've got to decide that reliable news and information is as at least as worthy as Starbucks of our daily tithing. Which brings us to the next gap.

The Chump Gap. It took Walter Isaacson, former editorial director of Time Inc. and CEO of CNN News, to identify this one for us. Isaacson got *Time*, his old embattled employer (newsmagazines, ironically, may be the only news category in worse shape than newspapers) to put his incendiary call to action, "How to Save the Newspaper," on a February 2009 cover. He made a number of points about journalism's societal value and came to the conclusion that the news media needed—somehow—to charge online. How? He wasn't sure. But he was one of many people to express alarm.

Here's the kicker. He told us that since *The New York Times*, a great paper he acknowledged, was free on the Web, he wouldn't pay for it in print. Why? He didn't want to be a chump!

We owe Walter for identifying the Chump Gap. How many of you have said to yourself, family, or friends, "I don't know if I should cancel the daily [print] paper. We don't read it as much anymore, and we can get it online, right? Is that okay, the right thing to do?" I hear these qualms all the time—and often from people in or close to the business.

It's an absolutely fair question.

Here's the problem. We'll all end up getting the quality of news and information that we pay for. We can't leave that quality—and quantity—to the vagaries of how the digital ad revolution plays out. First off, no one has any idea how much money the new ad businesses will throw off. Secondly, as we've seen throughout Newsonomics, the fortunes of the ad business have gotten disconnected from the news business.

So, I think that leaves us saying, I'm not a chump, I'm a champion. Just as we pay for cable programming and broadband Internet and support all kinds of community and global organizations, we can support news and information. No, it doesn't have to mean throwing some dimes in a tin cup. It means stepping forward and proudly proclaiming your financial support, especially for community and investigative journalism. MinnPost is testing this ground, with some acceptance, but I fear many civic-minded Minnesotans are being held back by the Chump issue. This is a gap any and all of us can close with our words and our wallets, if—and this is a big if—news organizations give us the opportunity to build and rebuild them. The non-profits and journalism-first, for-profit start-ups can make this appeal better than the Sam Zells and Dean Singletons.

The Skills Gap. We've seen this is the new Darwinian age of content. We also see a bit of Darwin's natural selection under way in newsrooms across the world. For more than a decade, too, many journalists hemmed and hawed when offered the ability to step out of their comfort zones, to blog, to shoot video, and even to record interviews. Newsroom managers, with some exceptions, enabled such behavior.

Today, the skills gap makes playing catch-up all the harder as budgets shrink. So, those with flexible skills and attitudes are ascendant in the industry, while those without them are seeing careers suddenly ended. With more than 200,000 students in U.S. communications and journalism schools eagerly ready to accept lower wages to get a start in the news trade, the incumbents have little choice remaining: Learn quickly or leave.

The Management-Labor Gap. When I served as managing editor of the *Pioneer Press*, we completed a major restructuring of the newsroom. It made sense to me to thoroughly involve the staff in that work, and we appointed several committees to mush through the considerable questions and logistics. Arriving at work one morning, I got a call from Human Resources telling me that the Newspaper Guild was threatening to file an unfair labor practice complaint against me. My sin, I was told: According to the 1935 Wagner Act, only the Guild could appoint "workplace improvement committees." We weathered that storm without me being put on trial and, I think, we bettered the paper and the workplace.

The story reminds me of how much things have changed. The Newspaper Guild, now led by Bernie Lunzer, who worked in the *Pioneer Press* around that time, invited me to keynote its national conference last year. More important, the Guild now stands clear-eyed about the nature of the news industry, its challenges, and the tough choices it faces. It certainly stands up for its members; it has been a tough negotiator in the many downsizings in which it has been involved. Yet it now aims to become a better partner to news-producing companies—whoever may own them.

We—and I include the Guild here—have no idea what role organized labor may play given the new Newsonomics of the trade. This, though, is one gap that's been narrowed by necessity.

The Conversation Gap. All people get caught in the same old stories, in couples, in families, and in workplaces. Sometimes they are great and affirming stories, and sometimes they drag us down.

As soon as the Internet began to change news—as soon as the Excites of the world befuddled us all—news people focused their conversations on too many of the wrong things. The dance between what's published when, in print and online. The authority debates about what "print people" have, and what leeway to allow the "online people." Who has to do what when. The debates went on and on and on, and meanwhile the world developed around Old Media.

Now, many of those debates have been forced to closure by great financial stress. Yet consider the kinds of conversations that are still self-defeating. Let's just focus on three of the big relationship ones, but ones that affect and afflict almost all of Old Media.

Newspapers and AP. Daily newspapers own the Associated Press, and they've long had a love-hate relationship. The discord has turned to rebellion, given, again, financial stress, and the newspapers threaten to pull out of and blow up the co-op they own—and which could be one of their best, most efficient networks going forward.

Local TV Broadcast Affiliates and Their Networks. The push-and-pull here parallels the AP dysfunction and has prevented local stations from taking greater advantage of network efficiencies, while the networks themselves can only make limited use of their wider reach.

National Public Radio and Its 860 Affiliates. NPR should be perfectly positioned with its news style, its embrace of multimedia, its podcasts, and its Web site to compete well among the Digital Dozen. Instead, it has been wrecked by wholesale executive change, as the feud between national NPR and its largest affiliates holds it back.

Yes, it was hurt by the recession like everyone else, but decisions like the scaling back of NPR West should have been avoided, and could have been with more cooperation.

All these conversations, all these arguments, have good historical reasons to exist. Yet until the people and organizations involved get beyond them, they are tying one hand behind their back—and the new Newsonomics requires *at least* two.

The Bias Gap. One unexpected and unintended consequence of this digital information revolution: Anybody and everybody can be a publisher. Believing in free expression—right there in the predigital Constitution—that sounds great, and it can be.

The problem is that everybody can be a publisher. Pfizer is a publisher now, as are the CIA and Honda. Companies are not just changing where they put their ad dollars. They are going direct to customers, suppliers, and the public, without any messy intermediaries—and far fewer nosy journalists—between them and their audiences. There's nothing wrong with that, of course, but it's not journalism; it's publishing. Most of you reading this book immediately grasp that distinction; many of the one billion people worldwide online do not.

So there is a bias gap.

News people have always had a hard time explaining what they do and its value—witness those "integrity" numbers back in chapter 1 that rank journalists just above lawyers and actors. It would be great if universal civics classes successfully taught citizens how to distinguish among the sources of information, how to determine a source's self-interest, and why news people try to operate on a different fairness standard. That's not the world we live in, though.

That leaves us with a challenge—to restate what impartial news and information is all about—and to push for universal and standard placement disclosure on newsy Web sites about an organization's goals, standards, and funding.

The Fun Gap. Newsrooms are funny places, known for their gallows humor, often the best way to deal with what can be hard-to-withstand bad news. Yet the business has often sharply divided "hard" news from "soft" news.

I've seen the news business from at least six sides now—alternative press, monthly magazines, features, news, digital journalism, and analyst—and I can tell you tell that the divides that have long characterized the business are melting away.

Yet, in that meltdown, we see much chaos and questioning of self-identity. We see the gap exposed between old-style "Voice of God" journalism (as CBS executive Les Moonves once described the Evening News-anchor-gives-you-the-world notion) and the more free-wheeling, informal, blog-inflected world of news into which we are heading.

Blame Jon Stewart.

His *Daily Show* has been a mind-bending lesson for the mainstream news media. It's part deadly media criticism, a field long previously reserved for few select members of the brotherhood. It's part satire, high- and low-minded, off-the-news shtick. Increasingly, it has become big news itself. Nothing better symbolized this curious mixture than Stewart's week-long 2009 bashing of CNBC, its stock market cheerleading and often clueless role in the run-up to the financial meltdown. What began with the usual *Daily Show* feature, a film montage capturing and comparing statements over time, ended as "news" that swept far from the shores of *Comedy Central* back to all the big news networks, the *Times*, the *Post*, and news media around the world.

Stewart had seen the absurd—outrageous, repeated, and fact-lacking calls about stock market investing—and then proceeded to call CNBC on it. The word was "outrage," and within a few days, Jon Stewart had put a new face on how people were thinking and feeling about the great economic downturn. He'd given perspective and voice to something that had been nameless, but was plainly in the back of our minds.

The press also noticed he'd broken new ground in his early 2009 treatment of the media's coverage of Israel's invasion of Gaza. He took apart the often one-sided coverage of Israel by the U.S. press. As a Jew, he could make the case without opening himself up to the knee-jerk charges of anti-Semitism. As a comedian, he could show us the coverage's absurdity and make us laugh. As a press critic, he got attention—and made his viewers and news readers a little smarter, a little more attentive.

He is serious. He is funny. He is seriously funny. And it can all happen within any thirty seconds.

In so doing, he'd continued to make fun and make funny that gap between the serious and the laugh worthy. Stewart and his colleague Stephen Colbert have been a two-man crew bridging that Fun Gap. Late each night, they do the bridging, and during the day the rest of the media is coming around to similar notions.

It's a tough transition. Baby boomers have been largely confused by it. They came of age in a time of irreverence, but little of that got into the news products they produced. They have held sway at traditional news organizations for years, but they've largely maintained the traditional walls they inherited. Hard news in A, metro, and business sections and at the top of the evening news. Features, entertainment, and sports in separate sections or later in the broadcast.

In old-line newsrooms, the only time you'd hear actual chortling on the copy desk is when the Dave Barry column moved over the wires, but despite his early Stewart-like take on the absurdity of big and important (as well as silly) things, his column was safely dispatched to the lifestyle pages.

Now things are changing greatly.

Public radio—listened to by more than 25 million people a week—has helped close the Fun Gap. *All Things Considered* will give you heartbreaking, on-the-ground reports from China's devastating earthquake in one segment and then follow up with a feature on yodeling. It doesn't seem jarring; it just seems to follow how life really works. The listeners get it. They love the musical backgrounds and interludes, the occasional satire, and the honest, direct conversations they often hear with NPR and other Old Media correspondents, personally and intimately describing what they've experienced.

Newspapers and broadcasters have been slower to bridge the Fun Gap.

They hear a little Voice of Objectivity whispering in their ears. Objectivity is an artifact of monopoly journalism, aided and abetted by academics who thought it sounded like a good idea.

You all know objectivity: Get two sides of every question. He said. She said. Equal treatment. As an abstract idea, it impressed. For

readers wanting to know just what the hell is going on, it is seriously lacking. The daily press grabbed on to objectivity as it turned
monopolist—after World War II—in city after city. Before then, the
press had been more opinionated, often more partisan: think of the
style of the cable news stations and talk radio today, in part. Readers
tended to pick the publication by its tone as much as by anything else.
As single dailies came to dominate city after city, editors felt the weight
of their increased responsibility. They were often the sole arbiter of
the biggest news of the day. They really were gatekeepers.

So, too many decided that sticking a microphone—literal or
figurative—in front of two opposing viewpoints would tell the readers what they needed to know. They were wrong. Readers, viewers,
and listeners want fairness, not equal time. They want to understand
events and issues.

We come full circle to the reader revolution that the digital age
has birthed.

The Internet has broken the shackles of monopoly journalism for
all of us. It has truly made us our own editors. We're no longer tied
to "subscribing" to single products to get the news. We've bridged
our own gaps all by ourselves, as we choose the Old Media, start-up
site, blog, and podcast we want. We can change them at a moment's
notice and tout the best to those in and near our lives, in the next
room or 10,000 miles away. From Politico to Huffington Post to NYT
blogs to the new "Heard on the Street" and SlateV, we see a greater
willingness among journalists to express what they actually see in
front of them, rather than falling back on trite formulas.

That's the new world of news.

As the Digital News Decade begins, we stand in wonder of what's
possible, and we worry about what's not being reported. The Laws
of Newsonomics we've toured will determine much of both, and we,
as citizens and readers, must help make these new news economics
work in *our* favor.

Index